Muffins from the Heart

By SHIRLEY MARIE HARTUNG
First Printing

Typeset by Kim Vivian

Design and Printing by
Allprint Ainsworth Associates Inc.

Cover Photography by the Ontario Milk Marketing Board

Sketches by Doug Hartung

Copyright by: S. M. Hartung

Published by: Cookies Naturally
                          32 Layton St.
                          Kitchener, Ontario

Printed in Canada by: Allprint Ainsworth Associates Inc.
                          Kitchener, Ontario

Nutritional Analysis by: LeeAnne Kidd, R.P.Dt.

Sketches by: Doug Hartung

ISBN 0-9694115-1-0

The information and directions in this book are in no way to replace those given by medical and health professionals. You should discuss any major changes in your diet first with such a professional.

Cover photo compliments of the Ontario Milk Marketing Board.

This book is dedicated

- to my mother, a gifted cook, who is happiest when working in her kitchen
- to my father, for his gift of hospitality, according to whom "second helpings" are a must

This book is also dedicated to the Lord, the giver of all good gifts.

Thanks

- to the Milk Marketing Board for the cover photography
- to the McNeil Consumer Products Company for their contribution of Splenda for testing the diabetic recipes
- to my Mother for re-living her childhood memories, so I in turn could share them with you in story form
- to my nutritionist LeeAnne Kidd for the pleasure she was to work with
- to my friends at Kaufman Y for their support
- to my husband Doug, and son Shawn, my best friends and most valued critics

&&&

In Memory

**This book is in loving memory of my Grandmother
Maggie Love
for her hard work and ingenuity;
a woman, who today would be considered
physically challenged.**

Introduction

Although this book is about good health, it is not just about being good to your physical body. It is also about being who you really are and want to be by listening to and following your heart.

When I first made the decision to give up teaching to go back to writing cookbooks, the reactions were interesting.

"You're giving up teaching to test recipes?"
"During the recession?"
"Are you crazy?"

The answers to these questions were:

"Yes."
"Yes." and
"Probably."

Then I had the opposite reaction which was more positive, although maybe not always as realistic.

"You're giving up teaching to write another cookbook?"
"That's great!"
"It must be so exciting!"
"I've always wanted to... BUT ...!"

My response to this was, "Go after your dream." Even though following your heart means hard work, ingenuity, risk-taking and often financial sacrifice.

This book is the result of following a dream. Luckily, my husband and son have been my key supporters. I persisted, and they with me, and so here it is — proof that you too can realize your dream, whatever it might be. I am proud and excited to present to you,....

Muffins From The Heart!

Shirley Hartung

Nutrition Statements

- The recipes in this book have been designed for good nutrition. Other than the 'special occasion' recipes, these muffins generally have considerable fibre, and a controlled sweet and fat content. For heart-healthy muffins avoid recipes using coconut, use egg whites or alternative (see pg. 78 for substitutions), low-sodium baking powder and the "no added fat" variation.

- "No added fat" does not mean that the muffin is fat-free, but that it has had no fat added in the form of butter, oil or margarine.

- As the wheat-free variation is very similar nutritionally speaking to the basic whole wheat recipe, use the whole wheat analysis.

- Using Splenda to replace honey in the basic recipe is not significantly different with respect to diabetic food choices in comparison to using the reduced amount of honey, therefore use either product interchangeably. If you wish a slightly sweeter muffin use Splenda.

- As the gluten-free variation has so many flour choices and combination possibilities, and since the celiac is most interested in a gluten-free product, the nutritional analysis has been excluded for this variation.

- All recipes have been analyzed using the smaller amount of an ingredient if there is a choice. Nuts as an optional ingredient have not been included in the analysis.

- If desiring a high-fibre muffin, see the recipes labelled (H.F.)

- Please note: Since these muffins contain no preservatives, do not leave them unrefrigerated. If you wish to keep them for a longer period of time, they freeze very well if properly packaged.

Preface

I have always had a passion for muffins, but because of the number of muffin cookbooks already on the market, I have hesitated to add yet another to the list. When my heart finally won the battle, I knew that this book would have to be unique. I have tried to accomplish this in several ways, such as addressing various health issues.

The basic recipes contain high fibre, low-sodium wholesome ingredients with alternatives for those requiring a wheat-free, gluten-free, diabetic, no-added fat variation, or a combination of these variations.

Yields, as well as the nutrient analysis for each recipe are based on the *large size which requires 1/2 c. batter,* with the exception of the *carbohydrate-reduced variation, which requires 1/4 c. batter* per muffin. Diabetic choices are also included for this variation. The mega size requires 1 c. batter and is a meal in itself. The nutrient analysis is also based on the smaller amount of an ingredient if there is a choice e.g., 1/4-1/2 c.

Bake the mega size for 30-35 minutes,(I have indicated those that definitely take only 30 min.) Bake the large size for 25-30 minutes. The gluten-free variation requires 10-15 minutes longer and reduce heat 25º. Bake diabetic muffins approximately 15 minutes. Note: These times may vary with your oven.

For those with food sensitivities, I have included a section at the back of the book with alternative suggestions. These are categorized under specific foods, such as flour and sugar substitutes, etc.

All recipe variations have been tested many times.

Nutritional and time-saving tips have been included through-out the book and, in case you would rather read than bake, I've shared some home-spun stories with you, that may brighten your day.

It is my hope that *"Muffins From The Heart"* will become a companion in your kitchen. May the pages be worn with use and your compliments be many. If this is the case, it will all have been worthwhile following a dream!

Shirley Marie Hartung

A Special Word to:

THE WHEAT SENSITIVE — all recipes suitable for the wheat-sensitive have been tested using a flour mixture consisting of equal amount of rye, oat and barley. You can buy this flour pre-mixed which is convenient. However, if sensitive to one of these grains you will have to mix your own, replacing the offending grain with a suitable alternative.

Spelt, one of the oldest grains known to man, provides another possibility for most who are sensitive to wheat. As its nutrition is concentrated in the inner kernel of the grain, this is not lost during the milling process as is often the case. Also, due to the high water-solubility of Spelt, the body is able to absorb its nutrients with minimum strain on the digestive system. Its high concentration of protein is sufficient for normal daily requirement and it has more fibre than wheat, so is a good choice for those requiring a higher fibre diet. A special carbohydrate in Spelt known as monopolysaccharides stimulates the body's immune system, thereby helping to fight infection.

Buckwheat or barley may also replace wheat and each is less expensive than Spelt. Contrary to what the name implies, buckwheat is not a wheat. In fact it isn't even a grain but is a member of the rhubarb family. It is also high in fibre and contains a high-quality protein. Choose the lighter-coloured flour if you prefer a less distinctive flavour.

Regular natural bran is replaced with *oat bran* or *oatmeal* in this variation. A combination of the two could also be used. This variation sometimes requires less liquid. This is indicated where applicable. Although the muffins do not always rise as high as the basic whole wheat recipe, I am generally very pleased with the results of this variation.

THE FAT CONSCIOUS — in the "no added fat" variation, oil has been replaced with unsweetened applesauce. Although the muffin is heavier, it is still quite acceptable. If you wish to replace only half the oil with applesauce, this could be done. However, because I have tried to keep the oil content low in my recipes, this would probably only be a worthwhile consideration for a recipe such as The Ready Molasses Bran Mix which has a larger yield. I omit the use of nuts in this variation as they increase fat content considerably.

THE CARBOHYDRATE CONSCIOUS — in the carbohydrate-reduced variation, the size of the muffin has been altered so it is appropriate for the diabetic. I have tested the recipes using small amounts of honey as well as the newest sweetener replacement — Splenda. Since it is the total carbohydrate content that is important, rather than the type of sweetener used, either choice is appropriate. Diabetic choices have been supplied for recipes using this variation. Unsweetened applesauce has been used in this variation as well to replace the oil, as weight is sometimes a consideration for the diabetic. Because Splenda is very low in calories (2 calories/tsp.), you can use as much as indicated for the honey in the basic recipe and still stay within the safety margin. For best results choose those recipes with moist ingredients.

THE GLUTEN SENSITIVE — of all the variations I tested, this without question, was the most challenging. I have tested many different flours and combinations of flours. What I have indicated that I have used in a recipe, may not be your favourite choice so simply choose another of the options listed at the back section of the book under substitutions. For both convenience and economy, I prefer to use a combination of rice flour and a starch — cornstarch, tapioca, or arrowroot. (See substitution section for ratios for these and other combinations.) Brown rice flour has a stronger smell than white rice flour and it seems more gritty. Consequently, you may prefer to combine the two kinds. Soy flour also has a stronger smell. I prefer to use it in small amounts and in combination with other gluten-free flours.
For convenience you can use a commercially prepared mix or make your own. (see pg. 84)

Although I have tested all recipes that were possible to make gluten-free, those high in moisture and fruits or vegetables, or a combination of these such as Rise and Shine pg. 40, are definitely superior.

As gluten-free flours often produce a dry product, I have used buttermilk in place of regular milk to add some richness to this mixture. Plumped fruits add extra moisture to gluten-free muffins. Remember also, that you must use a gluten-free baking powder. Again, you can buy commercially prepared or make your own. (see pg. 85).

Tips for Preparing and Baking Gluten-Free Mixtures:

1   Decrease baking temperature by about 25ºF.

2   Increase baking time briefly (10-15 minutes).

3   Put a pan of water in the bottom of the oven so there is some moisture in the oven.

4 Allow the batter to sit covered in the refrigerator for at least a half hour before baking. This is especially important for a rice flour mixture as otherwise it becomes too hard when baked.

5 Choose recipes with moist ingredients for best results.

6 Immediately after cooling, wrap, place in a well sealed container, label and store in freezer.

7 Use dull or dark pans, not shiny ones.

8 A banana helps bind the mixture together.

9 Applesauce adds moisture, while cream cheese adds richness as well as binds the mixture.

10 Fruits with acid, such as pineapple and rhubarb, help to break down the gritty nature of brown rice flour.

11 Plump dried fruits by soaking in hot water several hours until fruit expands.

12 Pureed unsweetened canned or fresh stewed fruit, may be used in place of part or all of the liquid.

13 Guar Gum helps to bind the ingredients (use approx. 1-2 tsp./recipe)

Warning — as celiacs can become seriously ill if an ingredient is used that contains gluten, it is the responsibility of the individual to ensure that all products used are gluten-free. Some foods normally considered safe such as dried fruits, nuts and seeds may be dusted with flour.

Whole Bean Flour is made from romano beans. This flour absorbs more liquid so recipes have to be adjusted somewhat. I use one less cup of flour but do not alter the liquid. Again, I prefer to combine with a starch using 75% flour 25% starch.

Chick-Pea Flour — another legume flour that can replace a small amount of total flour used (1/4 the total amount).

Amaranth — Another gluten-free flour is made from a seed and is another choice for a grain-free product. It has many of the excellent cooking properties of wheat without the gluten. It is a more expensive flour to use.

EQUIPMENT — Very little equipment is needed beyond your basic kitchenware to prepare these recipes, however, I find the following items helpful:

1. A food processor or good blender to mix liquid ingredients quickly.

2. A mincer of some type which will mince whole fruits, e.g. oranges

3. An oven thermometer to check accuracy of oven temperature

4. A food processor with a shredder blade to shred carrots, apples, etc.

5. A 1/8 cup measuring spoon is needed for some gluten-free recipes.

6. A cake tester for checking doneness.

7. A "jumbo" muffin tin if you wish to make "mega" muffins. These come in different sizes. The one I have used to get the yields listed has only 6 mold to a tin. Each mold measures 4 inches across and 2 inches deep.

8. A couple of mini loaf tins or rectangular pyrex casserole dishes for left-over batter as some mega recipes make 8 rather than 6 mega muffins. The casserole I use measures 4 inches across and 2 1/2 inches deep and works perfectly. *Note:* Batter may be baked in regular loaf pans if so desired.

Table of Contents

Table of Contents

Type of Muffin

Table of Contents

Apple Sesame Muffins (H.F.)

375°F — 30 min. for mega size　　　　　　　　(no milk variation)
(Use a good cooking apple for this recipe such as Ida Red.)

4 c. whole wheat or wheat-free flour
1 1/2 c. natural bran (oatmeal for wheat-free)
1 tbsp. baking powder
2 tsp. baking soda
2 tsp. cinnamon
1 c. washed, dried raisins (1/2 c. for diabetic)
1 c. sesame seeds
2 c. skim milk or unsweetened apple juice
3/4 — 1 c. liquid honey (1/3 c. for diabetic)
1/2 c. canola oil or unsweetened applesauce
2 large eggs or equivalent egg substitute
2 c. peeled, chopped apples (2 large apples)

Preheat oven to 375°F. Mix together flour, bran or oatmeal, baking powder, baking soda and cinnamon. Stir in raisins and sesame seeds. Beat together milk or juice, honey, oil or applesauce and eggs or egg substitute. Peel, core and chop apples. Stir apple chunks into liquid mixture. Add liquid mixture to dry ingredients, stirring only until blended. Fill prepared muffin tins, the size of your choice and bake accordingly. (see pg. 6) If desired, sprinkle bottom and sides of muffin tins with sesame seeds before filling with batter.

Gluten-Free: not appropriate

Yields & Nutrient Analysis for Large & Carbohydrate-Reduced Sizes:

	Yield	Energy (Kcal)	Protein (g)	Fat (g)	Carb. (g)
Whole Wheat/Regular	15	394	10.5	15	61.7
No Added Fat	17	290	9.3	6.5	55.2
Carbohydrate-Reduced	35	115	4.4	3.1	20
Diabetic Food Choices	1 starch + 1/2 Fruits/Vegetables				

NUTRITIONAL TIP: Most seeds are rich in phosphorous, but poor in calcium, however, sesame seeds if purchased unhulled, have twice as much calcium as phosphorous. They are packed with vitamins, minerals, calcium, iron and protein. The mucilage content provides soothing qualities and the lecithin lowers the level of cholesterol.

Other good cooking apples are Spartan, Spy or Granny Smith if you wish a green apple.

Cheesy Cheddar Apple Muffins

350ºF
(Apples are always best with cheese.)

4 c. whole wheat or wheat-free flour
3 tsp. baking powder
1 1/2 tsp. baking soda
1 tsp. cinnamon
1/2 tsp. nutmeg
1 c. shredded sharp cheddar cheese
1 c. unsweetened apple juice (3/4 c. for celiac)
3/4 c. liquid honey (1/4 c. for diabetic)
1/4 c. canola oil or unsweetened applesauce
3 large eggs or equivalent egg substitute
2 c. peeled, shredded apple (2 large apples)

Preheat oven to 350ºF. Mix together flour, baking powder, baking soda, cinnamon and nutmeg. Stir in shredded cheese. Beat together juice, honey, oil or applesauce and eggs. Stir in shredded apple. Add liquid mixture to dry ingredients, stirring only until blended. Fill prepared muffin tins, the size of your choice and bake accordingly. (See pg. 6)

Gluten-Free: yield 13 (using rice/arrowroot combination, see pg. 84)

Yields & Nutrient Analysis for Large & Carbohydrate-Reduced Sizes:

	Yield	Energy (Kcal)	Protein (g)	Fat (g)	Carb. (g)
Whole Wheat/Regular	12	321	10	10	50
No Added Fat	13	258	9	4.8	47
Carbohydrate-Reduced	28	105	4.3	2.3	17.8
Diabetic Food Choices	1 starch				

TIP: Measure oil before honey, the honey will then slide easily out of the measuring cup — no spatula necessary!

Chunky Apple Muffins

350ºF — 30 min. for mega size   (no milk variation)
(Serve warm with a chunk of cheese.)

2 c. whole wheat or wheat-free flour
2 c. regular oatmeal
1 tbsp. baking powder
2 tsp. baking powder
2 tsp. baking soda
1/4 — 1/2 tsp. nutmeg
1/2 c. washed, dried raisins
1/2 c. chopped walnuts (optional)
1 c. skim milk or unsweetened apple juice
1/2 — 3/4 c. liquid honey (1/3 for diabetic)
1/4 c. canola oil or unsweetened applesauce
2 large eggs or egg substitute
2 c. apple chunks (2 medium to large apples)

Preheat oven to 350ºF. Mix together flour, oatmeal, baking powder, baking soda and nutmeg. Stir in raisins and walnuts if used. Beat together juice or milk, honey, oil or applesauce and eggs. Peel, core and chop apples. Stir apple chunks into liquid mixture. Add liquid mixture to dry ingredients, stirring only until blended. Fill prepared muffin tins, the size of your choice and bake accordingly. (see pg. 6)

Gluten-Free: yield 12 (using "Gluten-Free Anytime" Baking Mix and rice cereal, see pg. 84)

Yields & Nutrient Analysis for Large & Carbohydrate-Reduced Sizes:

	Yield	Energy (Kcal)	Protein (g)	Fat (g)	Carb. (g)
Whole Wheat/Regular	12	282	7.0	7.3	50
No Added Fat	12	242	7.0	2.5	51
Carbohydrate-Reduced	22	114	4.0	1.4	22.8
Diabetic Food Choices	1 starch + 1/2 fruits/vegetables				

TIP: Never overbeat your muffin batter or you will have a tough muffin with poor texture.

Oatmeal Applebutter Muffins

350°F
(An old-fashioned muffin with an old-fashioned flavour.)

1 c. skim milk or buttermilk
2 tsp. baking soda
2 1/2 c. whole wheat or wheat-free flour
1 1/2 c. oatmeal
1 tbsp. baking powder
1 tsp. cinnamon
1/4 tsp. nutmeg
1/2 c. coarsely-chopped walnuts (optional)
1/4 — 1/2 c. liquid honey (1/4 diabetic)
1/2 c. applebutter
1/4 c. canola oil or unsweetened applesauce
2 large eggs or equivalent egg substitute

Preheat oven to 350°F. Stir baking soda into milk and let sit while mixing the remaining ingredients. Mix together flour, oatmeal, baking powder, cinnamon and nutmeg. Stir in walnuts if used. Beat together honey, applebutter, oil or applesauce and eggs or egg substitute. Add milk with soda to this mixture. Add liquid mixture to dry ingredients, stirring only until blended. Fill prepared muffin tins, the size of your choice and bake accordingly. (see pg. 6)

Gluten-Free: yield 11 (using millet and tapioca combination in ratio as for rice and starch combination, see pg. 84 and rice cereal)

Yields & Nutrient Analysis for Large & Carbohydrate-Reduced Sizes:

	Yield	Energy (Kcal)	Protein (g)	Fat (g)	Carb. (g)
Whole Wheat/Regular	10	307	8.5	14.6	52.5
No Added Fat	11	235	7.7	2.8	48.2
Carbohydrate-Reduced	23	103	3.7	1.3	20.6
Diabetic Food Choices	1 starch + 1/2 fruits/vegetables				

For a nutritious, naturally-sweetened spread, use our own locally produced Wellesley applebutter or use it as an ingredient in your muffin as above.

Do's and Don'ts of Muffin Making

1. Muffins with a pointed top and coarse texture are a result of overmixing the batter. Work quickly with a light touch, mixing only until dry ingredients are moistened.

2. Flour fruits or nuts by adding to the dry ingredients. This prevents them from sinking to the bottom of the muffin.

3. Because whole wheat is heavier, it requires more leavener to rise. If this is a concern, use a low-sodium, aluminum-free baking powder or produce a lighter muffin by separating eggs, beat the whites, and fold these in after the other ingredients are combined. To replace the leaveners with yeast, use 1-2 packages per recipe. Add yeast and sweetener to lukewarm liquid and let sit 10 minutes. Add remaining combined ingredients to the yeast mixture. Bake 5-10 minutes longer.

4. Let baked muffins stand 5 minutes to firm up before removing from tins. This way they will come out all in one piece.

5. These muffins freeze well. Allow them to cool before wrapping and storing in an air-tight container.

Applebutter Autumn

Applebutter Autumn

Long, skinny fingers scratched against my window pane, arousing me from sleep. The few remaining leaves clinging to the big maple outside my bedroom window, rustled their message, "Get up, get up."

The smell of bread tickled my nostrils as the aroma floated up the back steps. Mother had been up for hours. I shivered as my toes touched the cold wooden floor. Hugging myself, I tip-toed to the window. Father was already loading the wagon. I had forgotten. Today we were going to the mill.

I dressed quickly, hurried down the back steps and rushed through the kitchen, letting the screen door slam behind me. As I reached the wagon, I heard Mother remind Father, "Don't forget the golden russets; they're good "cookers". I searched among the boxes. Mother, reading my mind said, "The snows are already loaded, dear."

"Hooray, we'll have fresh apple juice tonight." I knew, however, that the treat would be short-lived. The juice would ferment within a few days, the cold cement floor being our only refrigerator. We always got a big jug, none the less, as Mother would use the fermented juice to make cider vinegar needed for next pickle season. Mother always said, "nothing makes nine-day pickle like cider-vinegar".

To make the vinegar, Mother poured the fermented juice into a three-foot high, reed-covered, glass jug. She corked it after she added the shiny whitish blob of starter. The starter, which was called the "mother", began the size of a fifty-cent piece, but it would grow as it worked. Like "neighbour's yeast", it was saved and shared around. Mother strained the vinegar, with great care, through several thicknesses of cheesecloth to be sure that none of the "mother" was left in the vinegar. The story went, that if you got any in your stomach, it would continue to grow there and who knows when it would stop?

As I double-checked the wagon load for my own satisfaction, I was not, however, thinking about the "mother" or nine-day pickle, but of fresh, cool apple cider. "Are we getting apple syrup too?" I asked. Apple syrup (apple cider cooked down just as you would maple syrup) was a treat over hot biscuits, but my favourite was when we spread it on buttered bread, toasted over the red-hot coals of the dying embers of our wood stove. This was a bed-time snack sure to bring "sweet dreams". Mother had already packed the large stone crocks and gallon jars, ready to be filled.

Content that there were enough "snows" loaded, I ran to help Father carry the huge pumpkins Mother had grown in the garden. I swayed drunkenly under their weight. Father always liked pumpkin in his applebutter and it made the apples go further. I laughed out load as the mountains of pumpkins toppled over each other as Nellie and Queen rocked the wagon impatient to get going.

I jumped onto the seat beside Father. Mother handed me my red tin lunch-pail as Father flicked the reins. The mares needed no further prompting. We were finally off to the mill, our cargo of red, yellow and orange blending into the autumn landscape. It is because of memories like these that autumn is my favourite season. As I savour the applebutter on my warm muffin, my mind goes back to those autumns of so long ago and I am once again a little girl helping load the wagon. "Did you forget?" Today we go to the cider mill.

Shirley M. Hartung

     🍎 🍎 🍎

Speaking of applebutter, next time you come our way, why not stop into Wellesley, the applebutter capital? The village, about fifteen miles north-west of Kitchener-Waterloo, boasts the only remaining applebutter company left in Canada.

A.W. Jantzi and Son distribute their product across the country and they are rightly proud of their unique apple preserve. An old Pennsylvania Dutch recipe, the now famous Wellesley brand applebutter is a 100 per cent natural product. It contains no added sugar, preservatives, or artificial colour. What a refreshing surprise!

At least twenty-five tons of apples are required daily during peak season (September through January) to produce the applebutter and cider that we see on our supermarket shelves — that's a lot of apples. In fact, if all the apples used in a year were dumped over Wellesley, the village would be easily covered. Although there is no production during the months of July and August the store is open for business as usual.

The art of making applebutter began for Aaron Jantzi in the 1950s and the method has remained basically the same to this day. The equipment, however has been modernized. The company has expanded to include other products, such as applesauce and apple syrup, but make no mistake about it — Wellesley is applebutter!

Shirley M. Hartung

~meal Applesauce Muffins

~5°F
(no dairy)

(Applesauce makes this muffin moist.)

1 1/2 c. whole wheat or wheat-free flour
1 1/2 c. oatmeal
1 tbsp. baking powder
1 tsp. baking soda
1 tsp. cinnamon
1/4 tsp. nutmeg
1 c. cleaned, chopped dates (1/4 c. for diabetic)
2 c. unsweetened applesauce
1/2 — 2/3 c. liquid honey (1/4 c. for diabetic)
1/4 c. canola oil (omit for no added fat variation)
2 large eggs or equivalent egg substitute

Preheat oven to 375°F. Mix together flour, oatmeal, baking powder, baking soda, cinnamon and nutmeg. Beat together applesauce, honey, oil (if used) and eggs. Add chopped dates to the liquids. Add liquid mixture to dry ingredients, stirring only until blended. Fill prepared muffin tins, the size of your choice and bake accordingly. (see pg. 6)

Gluten-Free: yield 11 (using the "Gluten-Free Anytime" Baking Mix, see pg. 84 and rice cereal)

Yields & Nutrient Analysis for Large & Carbohydrate-Reduced Sizes:

	Yield	Energy (Kcal)	Protein (g)	Fat (g)	Carb. (g)
Whole Wheat/Regular	12	264	5.2	6.8	44.8
No Added Fat	12	222	5.2	2.1	44.8
Carbohydrate-Reduced	22	85	2.7	1.1	14.5
Diabetic Food Choices	1 starch				

Bake for 25 min.

Applesauce Bran Muffin (H.F.)

375°F
(Apple and bran — a good combination.)

2 c. unsweetened applesauce
1 1/2 c. buttermilk or low-fat sour milk
1/2 c. molasses or honey or 1/4 c. of each (1/4 c. total for diabetic)
1/4 c. canola oil (omit for fat-free)
2 large eggs or equivalent egg substitute
2 c. All-Bran cereal
2 1/2 c. whole wheat flour
3/4 c. wheat germ
2 tsp. baking powder
2 tsp. baking soda
1/2 c. washed, dried raisins (1/4 c. for diabetic)
1/2 c. coarsely-chopped walnuts (optional)

Preheat oven to 375°F. Beat together applesauce, milk, molasses and/or honey, oil if using and eggs. Combine this mixture with bran cereal and let sit while combining the other ingredients. Mix together flour, baking powder and baking soda. Stir in wheat germ, raisins and walnuts if using. Add liquid mixture to dry ingredients, stirring only until blended. Fill prepared muffin tins, the size of your choice and bake accordingly. (see pg. 6)

Gluten-Free: not appropriate

Yields & Nutrient Analysis for Large & Carbohydrate-Reduced Sizes:

	Yield	Energy (Kcal)	Protein (g)	Fat (g)	Carb. (g)
Whole Wheat/Regular	15	234	7.5	5.3	43
No Added Fat	15	202	7.5	1.5	43.7
Carbohydrate-Reduced	33	82	3.4	0.7	17.3
Diabetic Food Choices	1 starch				

Note: If using Splenda, add 1/4-1/3 cup extra milk.

Buttermilk Bran Muffins (H.F.)

350ºF to 375ºF
(You don't need boxed bran cereal in this recipe.)

1 c. natural bran or fine oat bran
2 c. buttermilk or sour milk
3 c. whole wheat or wheat-free flour
1 tbsp. baking powder
1 1/2 tsp. baking soda
1/4 — 1/2 c. canola oil or unsweetened applesauce
1/2 c. liquid honey (1/4 c. for diabetic)
4 large eggs or equivalent egg substitute
1 c. washed, chopped dates (1/4 c. for diabetic)

Preheat oven to 350ºF. Pour milk over natural bran (not oat bran). Mix flour, baking powder, baking soda and oat bran if used. Stir in chopped dates. Beat together oil or applesauce, honey, eggs and milk (if using oat bran). Add liquid mixture to dry ingredients, stirring only until blended. Fill prepared muffin tins, the size of your choice and bake accordingly. (see pg. 6)

Gluten-Free: yield 13 (using corn flour and corn bran)

Yields & Nutrient Analysis for Large & Carbohydrate-Reduced Sizes:

	Yield	Energy (Kcal)	Protein (g)	Fat (g)	Carb. (g)
Whole Wheat/Regular	12	272	8.1	7.8	38.3
No Added Fat	12	232	8.1	3.1	38.8
Carbohydrate-Reduced	26	87	3.6	1.4	12.5
Diabetic Food Choices	1 fruits/vegetables or 1 milk + 1 fruits/vegetables				

The
Real
Thing

The Real Thing

Buttermilk is a dieter's delight. Traditionally it was the thin, watery liquid left after churning. Today however, it is thick and creamy due to the culturing process. Because low-fat milk is used, it is an excellent ingredient choice. As well as being nutritious, buttermilk gives a light, tender texture to baked goods.

My grandmother, believing buttermilk to have medicinal benefits for those suffering stomach ailments, sent my mother across the fields to the next farm with a quart of buttermilk each time she churned. The ulcer, from which the neighbour suffered, may have been an indication that he never "struck it rich" while panning for gold in the Klodike.

&a &a &a

I have tried to keep the amount of fat in the recipes to a minimum, so that you may occasionally treat yourself to a warm "buttered" muffin. Mmmm.

Butter...it reminds me of the stories Mother tells of her childhood. She recalls, "during the war time, farmers made their own butter because it was rationed, so churning became one of my early morning chores. It was always cool churning in the cellar where the cream was stored. I hated that part of it, but Mother told me "Your job will be done all the sooner for it." Little did I realize at the time that the cool temperature helped the cream separate more quickly.

Together Mother and I would empty the contents of the fifty pound cream can through the opening into the large wooden bowl of the churn. (The bowl measured about a foot wide, a foot deep and two feet long) Before I started churning Mother always reminded me, "Make sure the lid is on tight, and check the plug." I understood the warning. The contents of the bowl were too precious to be spilled.

The churn stood a couple of feet off the floor and was mounted on rockers. I used the handles, positioned at one end of the bowl, to rock the churn, as you would a rocking chair. There was skill involved as the churn had to be rocked so that the cream would cut the figure eight.

As the slapping of the cream against the bowl was the only sound in the cellar, this was my make-believe time. I would pretend that I could hear waves echo against the shores of Hawaii or some other far-off exotic land that we had studied about in geography.

After about an hour of churning and day-dreaming, I would open the plug to let out the buttermilk, and then take the freshly churned butter out of the bowl. I had to rinse the butter and then press it with a wooden ladle to make sure all the liquid was out or it would go sour. The salt that I worked in by hand, gave the butter extra flavour. After filling the butter crock I would place it carefully in a box of fresh lime, which kept the butter from going rancid.

Dandelions, which cows grazed on in spring, gave yellow hue to the butter. In winter, a few drops of dandelion colour could be added to the cream to replace what spring had given naturally. If Mother didn't have any, she would cook up some carrots from the root cellar, mash them and use the juice to "yellow up" the butter.

As the butter melts into my freshly baked muffin, I taste it with a new appreciation. Although I have always considered butter a treat, I had never really understood the ease with which I can enjoy this luxury.

Shirley M. Hartung

Banana Bran Muffins (H.F.)

350°F — 375°F
(Potassium and fibre are the nutrition stars in this muffin.)

2 c. All Bran (oatmeal for wheat-free)
1 c. buttermilk
1/2 c. liquid honey (1/4 c. for diabetic)
1/4 c. canola oil or unsweetened applesauce
4 large eggs or equivalent egg substitute
2 tsp. vanilla
2 c. whole wheat or wheat-free flour
1 tsp. baking powder
2 tsp. baking soda
2 c. mashed, very ripe bananas (approx. 6)

Preheat oven to 350°F-375°F. Measure out bran or oatmeal. In a separate bowl, beat together milk, honey, oil or applesauce, eggs and vanilla. Pour liquid mixture over bran or oatmeal and let sit. In another bowl, mix flour, baking powder and baking soda. Mash bananas and add to bran mixture. Add banana bran mixture to dry ingredients, stirring only until blended. Fill prepared muffin tins, the size of your choice and bake accordingly. (see pg. 6)

Gluten-Free: not appropriate

Yields & Nutrient Analysis for Large & Carbohydrate-Reduced Sizes:

	Yield	Energy (Kcal)	Protein (g)	Fat (g)	Carb. (g)
Whole Wheat/Regular	12	249	7.5	7.4	43.5
No Added Fat	13	192	7.5	2.5	40.6
Carbohydrate-Reduced	29	79	3.1	1.1	16.3
Diabetic Food Choices	1 starch				

Chipper Bran Muffins (H.F.)

350ºF
(What a way to get your fibre!)

2 c. low-fat soured milk (leave milk sweet for diabetic variation)
1 tsp. baking soda
3 c. whole wheat or wheat-free flour
2 c. natural bran (oatmeal for wheat-free)
2 tbsp. baking powder
1 tsp. cinnamon
1 c. carob chips or chips of your choice (1/2 c. for diabetic)
3/4 c. liquid honey (1/4 c. for diabetic)
1/3 c. canola oil or unsweetened applesauce
3 large eggs or equivalent egg substitute
1 tbsp. vanilla

Let "Wheat-free" batter sit briefly to thicken, as it is rather runny when first mixed.

Preheat oven to 350ºF. Sour milk if necessary. Stir in baking soda and let sit. Mix together bran or oatmeal, flour, baking powder and cinnamon. Stir in chips. Beat together honey, oil or applesauce, eggs and vanilla. Add milk and baking soda mixture. Add liquid mixture to dry ingredients, stirring only until blended. Fill prepared muffin tins, the size of your choice and bake accordingly. (see pg. 6)

Gluten-Free: yield 16 (using bean flour/arrowroot combination, see pg 6 and corn bran)

Yields & Nutrient Analysis for Large & Carbohydrate-Reduced Sizes:

	Yield	Energy (Kcal)	Protein (g)	Fat (g)	Carb. (g)
Whole Wheat/Regular	15	281	7.3	8.3	47.0
No Added Fat	14	255	7.8	3.4	51.1
Carbohydrate-Reduced	28	98	3.8	1.8	19.4
Diabetic Food Choices	1 starch + 1/2 fruits/vegetables				

Analysis is done using chocolate chips as no nutritional information is available for carob chips.

TIP: To sour milk put 1-2 tbsp. vinegar or lemon juice in a measuring cup and fill with milk to measure 1 cup.

TIP: Carob chips can be purchased sugar and dairy-free. If using chocolate chips, avoid those containing palm oil.

Fig Bran Muffin (H.F.)

350°F
(I put figs in this muffin just for Dad.)

1 c. washed, chopped figs (1/2 c. for diabetic)
1 c. boiling water
2 c. All-Bran cereal (use oatmeal for wheat-free)
1 1/2 c. buttermilk
3 c. whole wheat or wheat-free flour
3 tsp. baking powder
1 1/2 tsp. baking soda
grated rind of 1 orange
1/2 c. coarsely-chopped walnuts (optional)
1/2 c. liquid honey (1/3 c. for diabetic)
1/4-1/2 c. canola oil or unsweetened applesauce
2 large eggs or equivalent egg substitute

Preheat oven to 350°F. Place chopped figs in water and bring to a boil. Then reduce to simmer. Soak bran or oatmeal in buttermilk. In another bowl, mix flour, baking powder and baking soda. Stir in orange rind and walnuts if using. Beat together honey, oil or applesauce, and eggs. Stir in softened figs and any remaining liquid. Combine liquid ingredients with bran or oatmeal buttermilk mixture. Add this to the flour mixture, stirring only until blended. Fill prepared muffin tins, the size of your choice and bake accordingly. (see pg. 6)

Gluten-Free: not appropriate

Yields & Nutrient Analysis for Large & Carbohydrate-Reduced Sizes:

	Yield	Energy (Kcal)	Protein (g)	Fat (g)	Carb. (g)
Whole Wheat/Regular	12	290	8.0	6.8	55.5
No Added Fat	12	250	8.0	2.0	56.0
Carbohydrate-Reduced	25	104	3.9	1.0	22.7
Diabetic Food Choices	1 starch + 1/2 fruits/vegetables				

Ready Molasses Bran Muffin Mix (H.F.)

375°F

(Muffins warm from the oven in minutes — a favourite.)

3 c. All-Bran cereal
3 c. natural bran (some oat bran may be used)
2 c. cleaned, chopped dates (1 c. for diabetic)
2 c. boiling water
4 c. buttermilk
3 tbsp. baking soda
1 c. canola oil or unsweetened applesauce
1/2 to 3/4 c. liquid honey (1/4 c. for diabetic)
1/2 to 3/4 c. molasses (1/4 c. for diabetic)
5 large eggs or equivalent egg substitute
5 c. whole wheat flour
1 tbsp. baking powder
1 c. chopped walnuts (optional)

Preheat oven to 375°F if baking immediately. In your largest mixing bowl, mix together All-Bran and natural bran. Stir in chopped dates and boiling water. In another bowl mix baking soda and buttermilk. Allow to stand. Meanwhile beat together oil or applesauce, honey, molasses and eggs. Mix flour and baking powder in another bowl. Add walnuts to flour mixture if using. Stir buttermilk mixture into bran mixture along with the honey mixture. Add flour mixture a few cups at a time to the bran mixture stirring only until blended. Fill prepared muffin tins, the size of your choice and bake accordingly (see page 6) or refrigerate mix in a sealed glass container for up to one month.

TIP: If using batter after being refrigerated, fill muffin tins as above, cover with wax paper and allow batter to come to room temperature before baking or muffins will not bake in time given, (especially the "mega" size and may burn if baking is extended too long beyond the suggested time). Top each muffin with a date before baking.

Gluten-Free: not appropriate

Yields & Nutrient Analysis for Large & Carbohydrate-Reduced Sizes:

	Yield	Energy (Kcal)	Protein (g)	Fat (g)	Carb. (g)
Whole Wheat/Regular	27	293	7.9	10.5	49.8
No Added Fat	25	241	7.9	2.1	55
Carbohydrate-Reduced	59	87	3.5	0.9	19.3
Diabetic Food Choices	1 starch + 1/2 fruits/vegetables				

Banana Mincemeat Muffins

350°F
(No need to wait until Christmas to make this muffin!)

2 c. of whole wheat or 2 1/2 c. wheat-free flour
1 c. natural bran or fine oat bran
1/2 c. wheat germ (omit for wheat-free)
1 tbsp. baking powder
1 tsp. baking soda
1/2 tsp. cinnamon
1/4 tsp. nutmeg
1/2 c. coarsely-chopped walnuts (optional)
1 c. low-fat milk
1/4 c. canola oil or unsweetened applesauce
1/4 c. liquid honey
2 large eggs or equivalent egg substitute
1 1/2 c. mincemeat (see pg. 76)
1 c. mashed ripe bananas (approx. 3)

Preheat oven to 350°F. Mix together flour, bran and wheat germ (if using), baking powder, baking soda, cinnamon and nutmeg. Stir in walnuts if using. Beat together milk, oil or applesauce and eggs. Blend in mincemeat and mashed banana. Add liquid mixture to dry ingredients, stirring only until blended. Fill prepared muffin tins, the size of your choice and bake accordingly. (see pg. 6)

Gluten-Free: yield 13 (using "Gluten-Free Anytime" Baking Mix, see pg. 84, corn bran and corn germ)

Yields & Nutrient Analysis for Large & Carbohydrate-Reduced Sizes:

	Yield	Energy (Kcal)	Protein (g)	Fat (g)	Carb. (g)
Whole Wheat/Regular	11	257	7.9	6.8	44.5
No Added Fat	12	195	7.3	1.5	41.3
Carbohydrate-Reduced	29	81	3.0	0.6	17.1
Diabetic Food Choices	1 starch				

Banana Pineapple Muffins

350°F   (no milk)

(An old favourite with a new twist.)

3 c. whole wheat or wheat-free flour
2 tsp. baking powder
2 tsp. baking soda
1/4 — 1/2 tsp. nutmeg
1/2 c. unsweetened coconut
1/4 — 1/2 c. canola oil or unsweetened applesauce
1/2 c. liquid honey (1/4 c. for diabetic)
2 large eggs or equivalent egg substitute
2 tsp. vanilla
2 c. mashed very ripe bananas (6 large)
1 c. drained, crushed unsweetened pineapple

Preheat oven to 375°F. Mix together flour, baking powder, baking soda and nutmeg. Stir in coconut. Beat together oil or applesauce, honey, eggs, and vanilla. Stir banana and pineapple into liquid ingredients. Add liquid mixture to dry ingredients, stirring only until blended. Fill prepared muffin tins, the size of your choice and bake accordingly. (see pg. 6)

Gluten-Free: yield 11 (using rice and starch combination, see pg. 84)

Yields & Nutrient Analysis for Large & Carbohydrate-Reduced Sizes:

	Yield	Energy (Kcal)	Protein (g)	Fat (g)	Carb. (g)
Whole Wheat/Regular	12	253	5.7	7.9	42.5
No Added Fat	12	212	5.7	3.2	43.0
Carbohydrate-Reduced	27	86	2.50	1.4	17.0
Diabetic Food Choices	1 starch				

Oatmeal Buttermilk Banana Muffins

375°F
(Buttermilk adds richness to this recipe without many calories.)

3 c. whole wheat or wheat-free flour
2 c. oatmeal
1 tbsp. baking powder
1 tsp. baking soda
1 1/2 c. buttermilk (1 c. for wheat-free)
1/2 c. chopped walnuts (optional)
1/2 — 2/3 c. liquid honey (1/2 c. for diabetic)
1/3 c. canola oil or unsweetened applesauce
4 large eggs or equivalent egg substitute
2 tsp. vanilla
1 1/2 c. mashed very ripe banana (3 very large bananas)

Preheat oven to 375°F. Mix together flour, oatmeal, baking powder, and baking soda. Stir in chopped walnuts if used. Beat together buttermilk, honey, oil or applesauce, eggs and vanilla. Stir in mashed banana. Add liquid mixture to dry ingredients, stirring only until blended. Fill prepared muffin tins, the size of your choice and bake accordingly. (see pg. 6)

Gluten-Free: yield 15 (using corn flour, and rice cereal)

Yields & Nutrient Analysis for Large & Carbohydrate-Reduced Sizes:

	Yield	Energy (Kcal)	Protein (g)	Fat (g)	Carb. (g)
Whole Wheat/Regular	15	266	8.0	8.3	42.7
No Added Fat	15	223	8.0	3.2	43.4
Carbohydrate-Reduced	32	100	3.7	1.5	19.2
Diabetic Food Choices	1 starch + 1/2 Fruits/Vegetables				

TIP: Although I prefer commercial buttermilk, buttermilk powder is also available and may be more convenient. To prepare, place 1/3 cup buttermilk powder in a measuring cup and fill with water to the 1 cup level. If you have neither the powder or the commercial buttermilk, use 1/2 cup low-fat yogurt and 1/2 cup low-fat milk to substitute for 1 cup buttermilk.

Old-Fashioned Banana Muffins

375°F
(Sometimes old-fashioned tastes best!)

3 c. mashed ripe bananas (approx. 6 large)
1 tsp. baking soda
4 c. whole wheat or wheat-free flour
2 tsp. baking powder
1/4 c. chopped walnuts (optional)
2 large eggs or equivalent egg substitute
1/4 c. canola oil or unsweetened applesauce
1/2 c. liquid honey (1/3 c. for diabetic)
2 tsp. vanilla

Preheat oven to 375°F. Stir soda into mashed banana and set aside. Mix together flour and baking powder. Stir in walnuts if using. Beat together eggs, oil or applesauce, honey and vanilla. Add baking soda and mashed banana mixture. Add liquid mixture to dry ingredients, stirring only until blended. Prepare muffin tins, the size of your choice and bake accordingly. (see pg. 6). TIP: Use over-ripe bananas as they are naturally sweeter.

Gluten-Free: yield 13 (using millet/arrowroot combination in ratio as for rice and starch combination, see pg. 84)

Yields & Nutrient Analysis for Large & Carbohydrate-Reduced Sizes:

	Yield	Energy (Kcal)	Protein (g)	Fat (g)	Carb. (g)
Whole Wheat/Regular	13	255	6.5	6.2	47
No Added Fat	13	218	6.5	1.8	47.4
Carbohydrate-Reduced	35	78	2.4	0.7	16.8
Diabetic Food Choices	1 starch				

TIP: Buy over-ripe bananas on sale and freeze in their skins for future use. To defrost, leave at room temperature until they are soft enough to mash. To hasten defrosting, run hot water briefly over frozen bananas or defrost in the microwave.

Hats Off to Maple Lane

Hats Off to Maple Lane

Trivia question — **What do Maple Lane Dairy and Peter Etril Snyder have in common?** True, both have a well-known business that started in Waterloo, but think again. Yes, both have also used horses in their chosen business. Maple Lane, when it first started, used horses to pull the milk wagons and Peter often used horses in his paintings. In fact, to this day, horses often find their way into Peter's well-known and appreciated art depicting local rural Mennonite life. Peter's love for horses started early in life. As a young child, he rode the horse-drawn milk wagons from the dairy owned by his father Etril, and his uncle Mel — the dairy being none other than Maple Lane.

Mel (Snyder) took over the dairy from Oscar Martin and Aldred Shantz in 1935, four years after they had started the dairy. Two years later, Etril became a partner with Mel, the two never dreaming of the success that it would become.

When Oscar and Alfred decided to begin a dairy in 1931, they called it Maple Lane Dairy as maple trees lined the lane of the Martin farm where the small processing plant was located. This brother-in-law duo started out with adjoining farms, four sons to help, twenty-five cows each and a 1923 Dodge touring car for deliveries, but not a single customer. This was soon to change and the dairy located on the Martin farm, north of Waterloo, was soon processing 350 quarts a day. This was quite an accomplishment for their small processing plant. However, today, modern technology allows Maple Lane Dairy to produce in excess of 400,000 litres of milk a day, as well as sell 40-60 other dairy and related products. In the beginning, the customer had only a choice of cream-top milk or pure cream.

When Mel and Etril bought into the dairy, it was moved from the Martin farm to a new plant located on King and Spring Streets in Waterloo, as it had outgrown the milk house. After seven years of business, they began to buy local dairies and over the next twenty years acquired many dairies from outside the area as well. In 1955, Maple Lane moved its entire operation to its present location at Lancaster and Breithaupt Streets in Kitchener, as there was no room to expand in Waterloo. With this move came the end of an era of horse-drawn milk wagons, as Maple Lane became the first area dairy to use refrigerated delivery trucks. Today, Maple Lane has a fleet of more than seventy trucks covering a two hundred mile radius. Prior to refrigeration, blocks of ice had kept the glass milk bottles cold, but with the introduction of the paper cartons in 1955, refrigeration was necessary as these cartons were not as good an insulator as the glass.

Eddy Cressman, a friend of the family who worked for the company, remembers when a quart of milk cost 12 cents. He also recalls that, during the war, the government paid the dairy a subsidy of 2 cents a quart, so the customer only paid 10 cents. We pay over ten times this amount today.

Mr. Cressman, who retired from the position of General Manager in 1987, related some humorous stories as he recently reminisced about his days at Maple Lane. One such story was when he was a rookie learning his route. One day as they began down the hill at St. Mary's Hospital, one of the backhold straps broke, (these straps kept the wagon from constantly hitting the horse). The two passengers jumped to safety, but not without scars and bruises. The horse kept running, constantly being hit by the out-of-control wagon. Half a mile and several turns later, the milk wagon was still upright, but the poor horse found herself feet-first under another Maple Lane wagon making deliveries on that street. The horse survived and was on the delivery route as usual the next morning.

Eddy recalls a fellow worker who arrived home particularly late on Christmas Eve. The overflowing hospitality of his customers had gone to his head, for he arrived back at the dairy in high spirits, riding rather than driving his horse.

Maple Lane has always been a leader in change. Not only did they have the first refrigerated trucks and the first milk cartons, they also were the first to use high temperature short-time pasteurization and the three-quart pitcher pak.

In 1960, Maple Lane was invited to join the Quality Chekd Dairy Products Association. This association is made up of 160 dairies who pride themselves on surpassing standards required by the departments of health and agriculture. Maple Lane is the recipient of the 1993 Quality Check Associations Award as the highest quality dairy plant in North America.

In 1970, Maple Lane joined Beatrice Food Inc. and so what started in the milk house of the Martin farm sixty-two years ago continues to grow and serve our community.

HATS OFF TO YOU, MAPLE LANE DAIRY!

Shirley M. Hartung

Blueberry Cream Muffins

375ºF
(This is a "cream of the crop" muffin.)

1 1/2 c. oatmeal
1 c. buttermilk (1/2 c. for celiac)
2 1/2 c. whole wheat or wheat-free flour
4 tsp. baking powder
1 c. fresh or frozen blueberries (if frozen, do not thaw)
grated peel of 1 orange
1/2 c. softened low-fat cream cheese (1/2 of an 8 oz. package)
1 c. unsweetened orange juice (1/2 c. for celiac)
1/2 c. honey (1/4 c. for diabetic)
3 large eggs or equivalent egg substitute

Preheat oven to 350ºF. Soak oatmeal in buttermilk. Mix together flour and baking powder. Stir in blueberries and peel. Beat together cream cheese, juice, honey and eggs. Add liquid mixture to dry ingredients, stirring only until blended. Fill prepared muffin tins, the size of your choice and bake accordingly (see pg. 6)

Gluten-Free: yield 9 (using corn flour, and rice cereal)

Yields & Nutrient Analysis for Large & Carbohydrate-Reduced Sizes:

	Yield	Energy (Kcal)	Protein (g)	Fat (g)	Carb. (g)
Whole Wheat/Regular	12	249	8.5	6.5	41.0
No Added Fat	—	—	—	—	—
Carbohydrate-Reduced	27	103	3.8	2.9	16.1
Diabetic Food Choices	1 starch				

Blueberry Peach Muffins

350ºF
(For variation, try a blueberry pineapple combination.)

3 c. whole wheat or wheat-free flour
2 c. oatmeal
1 tbsp. baking powder
1 tsp. baking soda
1/2 tsp. cinnamon
1/4 tsp. nutmeg
1 c. well-drained, chopped peaches (or pineapple chunks)
1 c. fresh or frozen blueberries (do not thaw if frozen)
1 c. low-fat milk (1/2 c. for celiac)
1/2 c. liquid honey (1/4 c. for diabetic)
1/4 — 1/2 c. canola oil or unsweetened applesauce
4 large eggs or equivalent egg substitute
2 tsp. almond extract

Preheat oven to 350ºF. Mix together flour, oats, baking powder, baking soda and spices. Carefully stir blueberries, and drained peaches or pineapple into dry ingredients. Beat together milk, honey, oil or applesauce, eggs, and almond flavouring. Add liquid mixture to dry ingredients, stirring only until blended. Fill prepared muffin tins, the size of your choice and bake accordingly. (see pg. 6)

Gluten-Free: yield 12 (using rice and arrowroot combination, see pg. 84 and rice cereal)

Yields & Nutrient Analysis for Large & Carbohydrate-Reduced Sizes:

	Yield	Energy (Kcal)	Protein (g)	Fat (g)	Carb. (g)
Whole Wheat/Regular	11	318	10.5	9.3	51.7
No Added Fat	11	274	10.5	4.1	52.3
Carbohydrate-Reduced	28	100	4.1	1.6	18.5
Diabetic Food Choices	1 starch				

Lemon–Blueberry Muffins

375°F
(Freshly picked blueberries taste best!)

4 c. whole wheat or wheat-free flour
1 tbsp. baking powder
1/4 tsp. cinnamon
1/8 tsp. nutmeg
grated peel of 1 large lemon or orange (1/2 for diabetic)
2 c. fresh or frozen blueberries (if frozen, do not thaw)
1 3/4 c. low-fat milk (1 c. for celiac)
2/3 c. liquid honey (1/3 c. for diabetic)
1/3 — 1/2 c. canola oil or unsweetened applesauce
2 large eggs or equivalent egg substitute
1 tsp. vanilla

Preheat oven to 375°F. Mix together flour, baking powder, cinnamon, nutmeg and peel. Carefully stir in blueberries. Beat together milk, honey, oil or applesauce, eggs and vanilla. Add liquid mixture to dry ingredients, stirring only until blended. Fill prepared muffin tins, the size of your choice and bake accordingly. (see pg. 6)

Gluten-Free: yield 10 (using rice/starch combination, see pg. 84)

Yields & Nutrient Analysis for Large & Carbohydrate-Reduced Sizes:

	Yield	Energy (Kcal)	Protein (g)	Fat (g)	Carb. (g)
Whole Wheat/Regular	11	326	8.9	9.2	56.3
No Added Fat	11	268	8.9	2.2	57.2
Carbohydrate-Reduced	25	104	3.9	1.0	21.6
Diabetic Food Choices	1 starch + 1 fruits/vegetables				

Blueberry
Daze

Blueberry Daze

Berries...they are on my mind today as I mix up another batch of blueberry muffins. The recipe, second nature to me by now, my mind begins to wander. It takes me back to a day in my childhood when Father took me to the Holland Marsh.

"Get your rubber boots on dear, we're going blueberry picking." Together we pulled on our high, black rubber boots and were off on our adventure. Hours later, we arrived home, my little tin honey pail almost full, and Dad's six quart baskets overflowing. The next day, fragrant and steaming hot from the oven, Mother's blueberry lattice pies made us appreciate Father's annual pilgrimage.

Mother, from her youth, learned to appreciate the bounty of nature; yet, being a typical kid, I'm sure that she would have preferred to play some days, than to go picking again. I remember her telling me, "Your Grandmother and I would go into the woods in the early morning to pick wild raspberries and would return after lunch with a twelve quart milk pail full, which we would then have to "do down". We always took along buttered bread to make raspberry sandwiches in case we got hungry. The woods was not Grandma's only resource for filling the large, cool, dark, white-washed fruit cellar. Her huge garden consisted of long, manicured rows of every imaginable vegetable. The fruit trees, which stood like sleeping wooden sentinels frosted with snow in winter, were fragrant with blossoms in spring. In summer, these same branches hung heavy with plums, peaches, pears, apples and

cherries. Black currants and gooseberry bushes were also part of Grandma's garden. These, along with the chokecherries, which grew wild along the rail fences made delicious jelly.

Since Grandma also grew grapes, come fall, there was always a jelly bag hanging in the kitchen. The crimson drops, filling the bowl below, would become grape jelly which was particularly delectable when spread on Grandma's yeasty, warm, home-made bread.

Since there were no strawberry plants started the year she was married in 1915, Grandma picked wild ones-fifteen pints of them which she found growing along the road, below the gate to their Southern Ontario farm. She also reports in her diary, "It was a bumper gooseberry crop this summer. I picked one hundred quarts off of my seven bushes and sold them for seven cents a quart (enough to pay for a "hundred" of sugar)".

As I gently stir another cup of blueberries into my muffin batter, I wonder about their story. Somehow the plastic tubs in which blueberries are sold today seem commercial and lacking in any mystery.

Each year, I plan to take my husband and son blueberry picking but somehow we've never done it. This year it will be a priority so we too, can add our story to those already being handed down to the next generation of berry-pickers.

Shirley M. Hartung

Carrot Pineapple *(Rise n' Shine Muffins)*

350°F

(A definite favourite but these take some work.)

3 c. whole wheat or wheat-free flour
1 tbsp. baking powder
2 1/2 tsp. baking soda
2 tsp. cinnamon
1/2 c. unsweetened coconut
1/2 c. washed, dried raisins
1/2 c. coarsely-chopped walnuts (optional)
1 tsp. grated orange peel (optional)
2 c. shredded carrot
1 c. well-drained unsweetened pineapple tidbits
1 packed c. shredded apple (press out extra juice if any)
3/4 c. liquid honey (1/3 c. for diabetic)
1/4 c. canola oil or unsweetened applesauce
3 large eggs or equivalent egg substitute
2 tsp. vanilla

Preheat oven to 350°F. Mix together flour, baking powder, baking soda and cinnamon. Stir in coconut, raisins and walnuts and peel if using. In another bowl, mix carrot, pineapple and apple. Beat together honey, juice, oil or applesauce, eggs and vanilla. Add carrot and fruit mixture to liquid ingredients. Add liquid mixture to dry ingredients, stirring only until blended. Fill prepared muffin tins, the size of your choice and bake accordingly. (see pg. 6)

Gluten-Free: yield 12 (using rice/cornstarch combination, see pg. 84, and 1-2 tsp. guar gum.)

Yields & Nutrient Analysis for Large & Carbohydrate-Reduced Sizes:

	Yield	Energy (Kcal)	Protein (g)	Fat (g)	Carb. (g)
Whole Wheat/Regular	16	222	4.6	6.3	39.4
No Added Fat	14	219	5.3	3.1	45.5
Carbohydrate-Reduced	26	102	2.8	1.7	20.3
Diabetic Food Choices	1 starch + 1/2 fruits/vegetables				

Carrot Prune Muffins (H.F.)

375°F
(A unique combination — why not give it a try?)

2 c. whole wheat or 2 1/2 c. wheat-free flour
2 c. fine oatmeal
1/2 c. wheat germ (omit for wheat-free)
2 tsp. baking powder
2 tsp. baking soda
1/2 tsp. cinnamon
1/4 tsp. nutmeg
1/2 c. coarsely-chopped walnuts (optional)
1 c. shredded carrot
1 c. pitted, chopped prunes (1/3 c. for diabetic)
1 c. low-fat milk
1/2 c. liquid honey (1/4 c. for diabetic)
1/4 — 1/2 c. canola oil or unsweetened applesauce
3 large eggs or equivalent egg substitute
2 tsp. vanilla

Preheat oven to 375°F. Soak prunes in boiling water to soften; meanwhile mix together flour, oatmeal, wheat germ, baking powder, baking soda, cinnamon and nutmeg. Stir in walnuts if using, carrots, and prunes. Beat together milk, honey, oil or applesauce, eggs and vanilla. Add liquid mixture to dry ingredients, stirring only until blended. Fill prepared muffin tins, the size of your choice and bake accordingly (see pg. 6).

Gluten-Free: yield 12 (using corn flour, rice cereal and corn germ)

Yields & Nutrient Analysis for Large & Carbohydrate-Reduced Sizes:

	Yield	Energy (Kcal)	Protein (g)	Fat (g)	Carb. (g)
Whole Wheat/Regular	11	299	10	8.5	47.8
No Added Fat	12	234	10	3.0	44.3
Carbohydrate-Reduced	24	101	4.5	1.5	18.0
Diabetic Food Choices	1 starch				

Black Gold

Louis Pellier was originally enticed to California by stories of gold but was unsuccessful as a prospector. He made his fortune in another kind of gold — *"black gold"*.

He started a nursery, and by grafting cuttings from prune plum trees from his native France to the rootstock of the wild American plum, he became the father of the United States prune industry.

Prunes, sun-ripened plums, are not only a natural way of keeping regular, but are also high in potassium, and a good source of vitamin A, niacin and iron. They are also a friend to the fibre-conscious.

Six prunes have more fibre than 2 servings (2/3 c. portions) of bran flakes and as much fibre as 4 slices of whole wheat bread, 6 peaches or 3 apples. They have no fat or cholesterol and each 1/4 c. has about 150 calories.

It's lucky for us that Louis struck it rich in "black gold".

Tip — To make prunes extra juicy, plump them by covering them with water and refrigerate over night. To prevent them from sticking to your knife, oil your knife blade before chopping them.

Lemon Zucchini Muffins

3 c. whole wheat or wheat-free flour
4 tsp. baking powder
1 tsp. cinnamon
1/2 tsp. nutmeg
1/4 tsp. ground cloves
2 tsp. lemon peel
1/2 c. coarsely-chopped walnuts or unsweetened coconut
1/2 c. cleaned, dried raisins or currants (1/4 c. for diabetic)
2 c. fresh or frozen shredded zucchini, drained and squeezed dry
1/2 c. unsweetened pineapple juice
1/3 — 1/2 c. canola oil or unsweetened applesauce
1/2 — 2/3 c. liquid honey (1/4 c. for diabetic)
4 large eggs or equivalent egg substitute
1 tsp. lemon or almond extract

Preheat oven to 350ºF — 375ºF. Mix together flour, baking powder, cinnamon, nutmeg, cloves and peel. Stir in walnuts or coconut, raisins or currants and zucchini. Beat together juice, oil or applesauce, honey, eggs and extract. Add liquid mixture to dry ingredients, stirring only until blended. Fill prepared muffin tins, the size of your choice and bake accordingly. (see pg. 6)

Gluten-Free: yield 10 (using rice/arrowroot combination, see pg. 84)

Yields & Nutrient Analysis for Large & Carbohydrate-Reduced Sizes:

	Yield	Energy (Kcal)	Protein (g)	Fat (g)	Carb. (g)
Whole Wheat/Regular	12	255	6.6	9.2	39.7
No Added Fat	12	201	6.6	2.8	40.3
Carbohydrate-Reduced	24	187	3.3	1.4	16.6
Diabetic Food Choices	1 starch				

Favourite Raisin Muffins

350ºF   (no milk)
(To save time, cook raisins the night before, cook extra and freeze.)

1 1/2 c. cleaned raisins
3 c. boiling water (reserve 1 c.) — omit for gluten-free
3 c. whole wheat or wheat-free flour
1 tbsp. baking powder
2 tsp. baking soda
1/2 c. liquid honey
1/3 c. canola oil or unsweetened applesauce
3 large eggs or equivalent egg substitute
1 tbsp. vanilla extract

Preheat oven to 350ºF. Cook raisins in boiling water for 15 minutes.
Cool in refrigerator. Drain, reserving 1 cup of liquid for the recipe. Save
the remaining juice, measure, label and freeze for another time. Mix
together flour, baking powder, baking soda and drained raisins. Beat
together honey, oil or applesauce, eggs, vanilla and reserved raisin
juice. Add liquid mixture to dry ingredients stirring only until blended.
Fill prepared muffin tins, the size of your choice and bake accordingly.
(see pg. 6)

Gluten-Free: yield 10 (using rice/starch combination, see pg. 84 and 1 tsp.
guar gum)

Yields & Nutrient Analysis for Large & Carbohydrate-Reduced Sizes:

	Yield	Energy (Kcal)	Protein (g)	Fat (g)	Carb. (g)
Whole Wheat/Regular	12	294	6.5	8.7	51.9
No Added Fat	12	240	6.5	2.3	52.4
Carbohydrate-Reduced	26	111	3.0	1.0	24.2
Diabetic Food Choices	1 starch + fruits/vegetables				

Fruity Muffins

3 c. whole wheat or wheat-free flour
2 tsp. baking powder
1 tsp. baking soda
3/4 — 1 c. unsweetened pineapple or orange juice (lesser amount
        for wheat-free)
1/2 c. liquid honey
1/4 c. canola oil or unsweetened applesauce
2 large eggs or equivalent egg substitute
1 whole orange minced (remove most of peel before mincing for
   diabetic)
1/2 c. washed, dried, minced raisins
1/2 c. finely-chopped dates

Preheat oven to 350ºF. Mix together flour, baking powder, and baking soda. Beat together juice, honey, oil or applesauce and eggs. Stir minced orange, raisins and chopped dates into liquids. Add liquid mixture to dry ingredients, stirring only until blended. Fill prepared muffin tins, the size of your choice and bake accordingly. (see pg. 6)

Gluten-Free: yield 10 (using rice/arrowroot combination, see pg. 84)

Yields & Nutrient Analysis for Large & Carbohydrate-Reduced Sizes:

	Yield	Energy (Kcal)	Protein (g)	Fat (g)	Carb. (g)
Whole Wheat/Regular	11	276	6.4	9.0	44.5
No Added Fat	11	233	6.4	3.8	45.1
Carbohydrate-Reduced	N/A	—	—	—	—
Diabetic Food Choices					

Go-Power Muffins (H.F.)

(Fibre is the word!)

3/4 c. washed, chopped apricots (1/4 c. for diabetic)
3/4 c. washed, chopped prunes (1/4 c. for diabetic)
3/4 c. boiling water
1 c. buttermilk
1 1/2 tsp. baking soda
2 1/2 c. oatmeal
1 1/2 c. whole wheat or wheat-free flour
2 tbsp. baking powder
1 tsp. cinnamon
1/2 tsp. nutmeg
1/2 c. coarsely-chopped walnuts (optional)
1/2 — 3/4 c. liquid honey (1/3 c. for diabetic)
1/3 — 1/2 c. canola oil or unsweetened applesauce
2 large eggs or equivalent egg substitute
1 1/2 tsp. vanilla

Preheat oven to 375°F. Wash, then chop apricots and prunes. Cook fruit in water while mixing remaining ingredients. Stir baking soda into buttermilk and set aside. Mix together flour, baking powder, cinnamon and nutmeg. Stir in walnuts if using. Beat together honey, oil or applesauce, eggs and vanilla. Stir in soda buttermilk mixture. Add liquid mixture to oatmeal. Stir in drained, chopped fruit. Add liquid mixture to dry ingredients, stirring only until blended. Fill prepared muffin tins, the size of your choice and bake accordingly. (see pg. 6)

Gluten-Free: yield 12 (using corn flour)

Yields & Nutrient Analysis for Large & Carbohydrate-Reduced Sizes:

	Yield	Energy (Kcal)	Protein (g)	Fat (g)	Carb. (g)
Whole Wheat/Regular	12	291	6.9	9.2	48.2
No Added Fat	12	238	6.9	2.8	49.2
Carbohydrate-Reduced	21	106	4.0	1.6	20.4
Diabetic Food Choices	1 starch + 1/2 fruits/vegetables				

Lemon Coconut Muffins

350ºF
(Serve this plain muffin warm, with a little marmalade.)

3 c. whole wheat or wheat-free flour
1 tbsp. baking powder
1/4 — 1/2 tsp. nutmeg
finely grated peel of 1 lemon
1/2 — 3/4 c. unsweetened coconut
1/2 c. coarsely-chopped nuts — walnuts, pecans or hazelnuts
    (optional)
1 c. buttermilk
2/3 c. liquid honey (1/3 c. for diabetic)
1/3 — 1/2 c. canola oil or unsweetened applesauce
4 large eggs or equivalent egg substitute
3 tbsp. freshly-squeezed lemon juice (omit for diabetic)
1/2 tsp. lemon extract

Preheat oven to 350ºF. Mix together flour, baking powder and nutmeg. Stir in lemon peel, coconut and nuts if using. Beat together buttermilk, honey, oil or applesauce, eggs, juice and extract. Add liquid mixture to dry ingredients, stirring only until blended. Prepare muffin tins, the size of your choice and bake accordingly. (see pg. 6)

Gluten-Free: not appropriate

Yields & Nutrient Analysis for Large & Carbohydrate-Reduced Sizes:

	Yield	Energy (Kcal)	Protein (g)	Fat (g)	Carb. (g)
Whole Wheat/Regular	9	364	9.4	14.3	53.6
No Added Fat	10	262	8.5	5.2	48.8
Carbohydrate-Reduced	21	109	4.0	2.5	19.1
Diabetic Food Choices	1 starch +1/2 fruits/vegetables				

Mixed Dried Fruit Muffins

350ºF

(A good back-packing muffin.)

1 c. cleaned chopped dates
1/2 c. cleaned chopped apricots
1/2 c. cleaned chopped currants
1/2 c. cleaned chopped raisins
1/2 c. dried peaches, pears or apple
1/2 — 1 c. boiling water
4 c. whole wheat or wheat-free flour
3 tsp. baking powder
2 tsp. baking soda
1/2 c. chopped walnuts (optional)
1 1/2 c. low-fat milk
1/2 c. liquid honey
1/4 c. canola oil or unsweetened applesauce
2 large eggs or equivalent egg substitute

Preheat oven to 350ºF. Soak dates, apricots, currants, raisins and pears in boiling water. Mix together flour, baking powder and baking soda. Stir in walnuts if using. Beat together milk, honey, oil or applesauce and eggs. Drain soaked fruits and add to liquids. Add liquid mixture to dry ingredients, stirring only until blended. Fill prepared muffin tins, the size of your choice and bake accordingly. (see pg. 6)

Gluten-Free: yield 15 (using corn flour)

Yields & Nutrient Analysis for Large & Carbohydrate-Reduced Sizes:

	Yield	Energy (Kcal)	Protein (g)	Fat (g)	Carb. (g)
Whole Wheat/Regular	14	306	7.8	5.8	60.8
No Added Fat	14	271	7.8	1.8	61.3
Carbohydrate-Reduced	N/A	—	—	—	—
Diabetic Food Choices	N/A				

Yogurt Date Muffins

350°F
(Yogurt, a highly nutritious food is sometimes called the friendly bacteria.)

3 1/2 c. whole wheat or wheat-free flour
2 tsp. baking soda
1/2 c. coarsely-chopped walnuts (optional)
1 c. skim milk yogurt
3/4 c. low-fat milk
1/2 c. liquid honey
1/4 — 1/2 c. canola oil or unsweetened applesauce
2 large eggs or equivalent egg substitute
1 c. washed, chopped dates (1/3 c. for diabetic)

Preheat oven to 350°F. Mix together flour and baking soda. Stir in walnuts, if using. Beat together yogurt, milk, honey, oil or applesauce and eggs. Stir dates into liquid mixture. Add liquid mixture to dry ingredients, stirring only until blended. Fill prepared muffin tins, the size of your choice and bake accordingly. (see pg. 6)

Gluten-Free: yield 12 (using rice/cornstarch combination, see pg. 84)

Yields & Nutrient Analysis for Large & Carbohydrate-Reduced Sizes:

	Yield	Energy (Kcal)	Protein (g)	Fat (g)	Carb. (g)
Whole Wheat/Regular	12	272	7.8	6.9	47.9
No Added Fat	12	231	7.8	2.2	48.3
Carbohydrate-Reduced	23	102	4.0	1.1	20.3
Diabetic Food Choices	1 starch + 1/2 fruits/vegetables				

TIP: Use tofu yogurt if sensitive to dairy-based yogurt.

Peachy Muffins

350°F   (no milk)
(Almond flavouring compliments the peaches.)

4 c. whole wheat or wheat-free flour
2 tsp. baking powder
2 tsp. baking soda
2 tsp. cinnamon
1/4 tsp. nutmeg
a dash of mace (optional)
1/2 c. coarsely-chopped walnuts (optional)
1/2 c. cleaned, dried raisins
1 c. unsweetened orange juice
2/3 c. liquid honey (1/3 c. for diabetic)
1/4 — 1/2 c. canola oil or unsweetened applesauce
4 large eggs or equivalent egg substitute
2 tsp. almond extract
2 c. coarsely-chopped fresh or frozen peaches, thawed and well
    drained (1 c. for diabetic)

Preheat oven to 350°F. Mix together flour, baking powder, baking soda, cinnamon, nutmeg and mace if using. Stir in walnuts if using and raisins. Beat together orange juice, oil or applesauce, eggs and almond flavouring. Stir peaches into liquids. Add liquid mixture to dry ingredients, stirring only until blended. Fill prepared muffin tins, the size of your choice and bake accordingly. (see pg. 6)

Gluten-Free: yield 15 (using bean flour & cornstarch with the 3 cup ratio in
    rice/starch chart, see pg. 84)

Yields & Nutrient Analysis for Large & Carbohydrate-Reduced Sizes:

	Yield	Energy (Kcal)	Protein (g)	Fat (g)	Carb. (g)
Whole Wheat/Regular	15	241	6.6	5.4	44.7
No Added Fat	15	209	6.6	1.6	45.1
Carbohydrate-Reduced	28	98	3.5	0.9	20.4
Diabetic Food Choices	1 starch + 1/2 fruits/vegetables				

TIP: To freeze peaches without sugar, fill an air-tight container within an inch of the top with sliced raw peaches and cover with unsweetened orange juice. Since fruit will darken if not totally covered with juice, cover with tin foil. Alternate method: Freeze peaches whole with skins on. Simply wash fruit, bag and freeze. To remove skins easily, blanch fruit by dipping briefly in boiling water, then place under cold running water. Skins will slip off easily.

Spicy Pear Muffins

375ºF
(Spices enhance this otherwise bland fruit.)

4 c. whole wheat or wheat-free flour
3 tsp. baking powder
2 tsp. baking soda
1 tsp. cinnamon
1/2 tsp. nutmeg
1 tsp. grated lemon peel
2 c. cubed, pears (3 1/2 – 4 fresh or drained, unsweetened
    canned pears)
1/2 c. cleaned dried raisins or chopped apricots or 1/4 c. of each
1/2 c. coarsely chopped walnuts (optional)
1 1/2 c. low-fat milk or unsweetened juice of your choice
      (1 c. for celiac, and wheat-free variations)
1/4 c. canola oil or unsweetened applesauce
1/2 c. liquid honey (1/4 c. for diabetic)
2 large eggs or equivalent egg substitute

Preheat oven to 375ºF. Mix together flour, baking powder, baking soda, cinnamon, nutmeg and lemon peel. Stir in pears, raisins, apricots and walnuts if using. Beat together milk or juice, oil or applesauce, honey and eggs. Add liquid mixture to dry ingredients, stirring only until blended. Fill prepared muffin tins, the size of your choice and bake accordingly. (see pg. 6)

Gluten-Free: yield 12 (using rice/starch combination, see pg. 84)

Yields & Nutrient Analysis for Large & Carbohydrate-Reduced Sizes:

	Yield	Energy (Kcal)	Protein (g)	Fat (g)	Carb. (g)
Whole Wheat/Regular	14	260	6.9	6.0	47.7
No Added Fat	13	242	7.4	2.0	51.8
Carbohydrate-Reduced	26	113	3.7	1.0	23.7
Diabetic Food Choices	1 starch + 1/2 fruits/vegetables				

Spring Tonic Muffins

375°F — 400°F   (no eggs)
(What else, but rhubarb!)

5 c. whole wheat or wheat-free flour
2 tsp. baking powder
2 tsp. baking soda
1 tsp. cinnamon
1/2 tsp. nutmeg
1/2 tsp. allspice
1/2 c. finely-chopped walnuts (optional)
3 c. chopped fresh or frozen rhubarb (press well to drain if using
    frozen)
2 c. buttermilk
1 c. liquid honey (1/2 c. for diabetic)
1/2 c. canola oil or unsweetened applesauce
1 tbsp. vanilla

Preheat oven to 375°F — 400°F. Mix together flour, baking powder, baking soda, cinnamon, nutmeg and allspice. Stir in walnuts, if using, and chopped rhubarb. Beat together milk, honey, oil or applesauce and vanilla. Add liquid mixture to dry ingredients, stirring only until blended. Fill prepared muffin tins, the size of your choice and bake accordingly. (see pg. 6)

Gluten-Free: yield 17 (using in rice/potato starch combination, see pg. 84)

Yields & Nutrient Analysis for Large & Carbohydrate-Reduced Sizes:

	Yield	Energy (Kcal)	Protein (g)	Fat (g)	Carb. (g)
Whole Wheat/Regular	16	268	6.6	9.3	45.2
No Added Fat	18	185	5.9	1.9	41.0
Carbohydrate-Reduced	34	85	3.1	1.0	19.2
Diabetic Food Choices	1 starch + 1/2 fruits/vegetables				

Pumpkin Raisin Muffins

350ºF
(Yields may vary depending on the use of canned or fresh pumpkin — canned is represented in yields below.)

3 c. whole wheat or wheat-free flour
1 tbsp. baking powder
2 tsp. baking soda
2 tsp. cinnamon
1 c. pure pumpkin
1/2 c. cleaned, dried raisins
1/2 c. coarsely-chopped walnuts (optional)
1/4 c. canola oil or unsweetened applesauce
2/3 c. liquid honey (1/4 c. for diabetic)
4 large eggs or equivalent egg substitute
3/4 c. low-fat milk

Preheat oven to 350ºF. Mix together flour, baking powder, baking soda and cinnamon. Stir in raisins and walnuts if using. Beat together pumpkin, oil or applesauce, honey, eggs and milk. Add liquid mixture to dry ingredients, stirring only until blended. Fill prepared muffin tins, the size of your choice and bake accordingly. (see pg. 6)

Gluten-Free: yield 11 (using millet and arrowroot in same ratio as rice/starch combination, see pg. 84)

Yields & Nutrient Analysis for Large & Carbohydrate-Reduced Sizes:

	Yield	Energy (Kcal)	Protein (g)	Fat (g)	Carb. (g)
Whole Wheat/Regular	12	261	7.3	7.6	44.5
No Added Fat	12	221	7.3	2.8	45.0
Carbohydrate-Reduced	24	90	3.6	1.4	17.0
Diabetic Food Choices	1 starch				

Eggcitement in the Hen-House

Eggcitement in the Hen-house

"The bantie rooster bit me behind my back," my sister announced indignantly. The pair of Japanese bantams, a gift to my sister and me, were not the perfect pets they were supposed to be. These black and orange feathered miniatures strutted around the farm as if they owned the place. Their personalities were surely at best, and they generally made life miserable for the two of us. Unfortunately they were just the beginning of our hardships with farm fowl.

However, the soft, yellow balls of fluff that arrived each year at Easter made up for those bossy bantams. Grandma used to raise her own chicks. The mother hens, known as "cluckers", would sit patiently by the hour on the dozen eggs or so that had been laid, getting up only occasionally to ruffle their feathers and stretch. The roosters never came near to help. Grandma always rubbed a little lard or butter on the necks of the mother hens to prevent them from giving lice to the chicks-which could lead to their demise. She fed them oatmeal, which they became quite fond of. What better way to start the day off?

We got our chicks from the hatchery as we needed too many to hatch or incubate on our own. As we carefully lifted the day-olds from their cardboard cartons, we were reminded, "Gentle, don't squeeze." Each compartment had been lined with excelsior-short thin shavings of soft wood, to make the trip as comfortable as possible. A little shaky at first, the chicks were soon exploring their new world with gusto. "Careful where you walk," Father reminded, little bodies darting all around. I giggled as one ran over the toe of my rubber boot.

As with all newborns, it was imperative to keep those little "peepers" warm. Initially the brooder stove took the place of their mother's warm body. When they were beyond the critical period, a heat lamp replaced it. When heat was no longer required, they were moved into the shelters.

This new residence featured a slanted roof and natural air conditioning. The slated floor was raised off the ground enough to facilitate air circulation. The slats, however, had to be close enough so that the chickens wouldn't get their feet caught or be pulled down through by some ravenous fox.

Mother would get up each morning at the break of day to let the chickens out of the shelter as they would pile up at the door clamouring to get out and would literally smother each other in doing so. Mother always said that they were the stupidest animals on the farm. When they were almost five months old, father would announce, "It's time for these chickens to go to work." So, under cover of night, we would sneak into the shelters and grab the unsuspecting chickens by the legs and carry them, half a dozen in each hand, to the hen house. The chickens never went peacefully. What a furor of squawking! When the chickens were new at egg-laying, the eggs were still small in size. They were called pee-wee eggs or pullet eggs. Soon they were practised and were laying regular-sized eggs. After laying about three hundred eggs a year, the hens would be layed out, especially if they had layed too many double yolkers.

Gathering all those eggs was not only a lot of work, but it was also dangerous. My sister and I joined forces against our feathered adversaries. Armed with the biggest stick we could find, we would enter enemy territory ready to whop the first rooster that would inevitably attack the moment one's back was turned. It was bad enough to be pecked by an offended hen who objected to being robbed, but to be attacked from both sides at once was too much to bear. When the nests had all been searched, we would make our exit as quickly as possible walking backwards, and carrying fragile merchandise.

Evidently, Grandma was detained in the hen-house one day as the ram attacked the door every time she attempted to leave. I'm not sure how long she was held captive, but knowing my grandmother's spunk, I'm sure that old ram lived to regret that day as did the old gander who found himself being flung by the neck over my grandma's head and over the fence after taking her on. That gander had met his match.

Although my little sister was too young to gather eggs, she and a little neighbour boy snuck into the hen-house and snitched some eggs for target practice. When asked why they were pelting eggs against the barn door, the neighbour boy tried to string mother some line about practicing his aim so he could catch that wild skunk that he had seen only yesterday. Oh well, I thought, fewer eggs to clean; but that's not what my mother said.

Another week we were short of our quota. Thinking I could save some time. I carefully tucked a basket of eggs under one arm, and with a heaping basket in each hand, began the slow descent down the barn steps. Half-way down, I realized that they were rather slick. It was too late and too precarious to turn back. Moments later I found myself at the bottom with egg on more than my face.

Once a week, Father would load up our new, blue '53 Pontiac and head off for the hatchery in Linwood. If he packed them just right, he could get in eleven crates. Sometimes I even got tucked in. Since each crate held thirty dozen eggs, it was important to avoid pot-holes and icy roads. Otherwise we might have had a contribution for "The Guinness Book of World Records", for the largest egg scramble, but little pocket money that week.

As I break another egg into my muffin batter, I begin to think that maybe I need a hen-house in my back yard. It would save a lot of trips to the store and I bet I haven't forgotten how to gather eggs either!

Shirley M. Hartung

🐦 🐦 🐦

DID YOU KNOW?
When it comes to packing a lot of nutrition into a small package, few foods can compare with eggs. In fact, in one large egg you will find most of the vitamins and minerals essential to health and an excellent source of high quality protein...All packed into just 75 calories.

"Good Morning" Museli Muffins

375°F
(We could call this a Swiss muffin because of the origin of Museli.)

1st Mixture:
3 c. museli cereal (see pg. 77)
1 1/2 c. unsweetened pineapple/orange or your favourite juice

2nd Mixture:
1 c. buttermilk or low-fat yogurt (1/2 c. for celiac)
1/2 c. unsweetened pineapple/orange or your favourite juice
1/4 — 1/2 c. canola oil or unsweetened applesauce
1/2 c. liquid honey (1/4 c. for diabetic)

3rd Mixture
2 1/2 c. whole wheat or wheat-free flour
1 tbsp. baking powder
3 tsp. baking soda

Pour juice over cereal and let sit overnight. Before baking preheat oven to 375°F Beat together buttermilk or yogurt, additional juice, oil or applesauce and honey. Add to soaked museli. Mix together flour, baking powder and baking soda. Add liquid mixture to dry ingredients, stirring only until blended. Fill prepared muffin tins, the size of your choice and bake accordingly. (see pg. 6)

Gluten-Free: yield 12 (using cornflour, and rice cereal, museli pg 77)

Yields & Nutrient Analysis for Large & Carbohydrate-Reduced Sizes:

	Yield	Energy (Kcal)	Protein (g)	Fat (g)	Carb. (g)
Whole Wheat/Regular	13	318	8.2	12.5	47.1
No Added Fat	13	281	8.2	8.2	47.5
Carbohydrate-Reduced	30	113	3.6	3.5	18.4
Diabetic Food Choices	1 starch				

Granola Muffins (H.F.)

350°F
(Breakfast in a muffin.)

4 c. whole wheat or wheat-free flour
2 c. homemade granola (omit dried fruits for diabetics see pg. 75)
2 tbsp. baking powder
1/2 c. washed, dried currants (1/4 c. for diabetics)
2 c. low-fat milk (1 1/2 — 1 2/3 c. for wheat-free)
1/2 c. canola oil or unsweetened applesauce
1/3 c. liquid honey
1/4 c. molasses (omit for diabetic)
2 large eggs or equivalent egg substitute
2 tsp. vanilla

Preheat oven to 350°F. Mix together flour, granola and baking powder. Stir in currants. Beat together milk, honey and molasses if using, oil or applesauce, eggs and vanilla. Add liquid mixture to dry ingredients, stirring only until blended. Fill prepared muffin tins, the size of your choice and bake accordingly. (see pg. 6) Top each muffin with a piece of dried apple and a handful of granola before baking if desired.

Gluten-Free: not appropriate

Yields & Nutrient Analysis for Large & Carbohydrate-Reduced Sizes:

	Yield	Energy (Kcal)	Protein (g)	Fat (g)	Carb. (g)
Whole Wheat/Regular	12	377	10.3	16.5	50.1
No Added Fat	13	348	9.5	6.5	47.6
Carbohydrate-Reduced	30	115	4.0	2.8	19.6
Diabetic Food Choices	1 starch + 1/2 fruits/vegetables				

Lemon Poppy Seed Muffins

350°F
(Poppy seeds contribute both eye appeal, and texture to this recipe.)

4 1/2 c. whole wheat or wheat-free flour
1 tbsp. baking powder
2 tsp. baking soda
3/4 c. poppy seeds
1 3/4 c. low-fat milk (1 1/4 c. for celiac)
grated rind of 1 -2 lemons (lesser amount for diabetics)
2/3 c. liquid honey (1/2 c. for diabetic)
1/2 c. canola oil or unsweetened applesauce (1/4 c. for diabetic)
1 1/2 — 2 tbsp. lemon juice
2 large eggs or equivalent egg substitute

Preheat oven to 350°F. Mix together flour, baking powder and baking soda. Stir in poppy seeds and lemon peel. Beat together milk, honey, oil or applesauce, lemon juice and eggs. Add liquid mixture to dry ingredients, stirring only until blended. Fill prepared muffin tins, the size of your choice and bake accordingly. (see pg. 6)

Gluten-Free: yield 12 (using the "Gluten-Free Anytime" Baking Mix, see pg. 84)

Yields & Nutrient Analysis for Large & Carbohydrate-Reduced Sizes:

	Yield	Energy (Kcal)	Protein (g)	Fat (g)	Carb. (g)
Whole Wheat/Regular	12	331	8.8	11.7	52.0
No Added Fat	13	229	8.1	2.0	48.4
Carbohydrate-Reduced	27	100	3.9	1.0	20.5
Diabetic Food Choices	1 starch + 1/2 fruits/vegetables				

TIP: To save unused freshly squeezed lemon juice, measure by tablespoons into an ice-cube tray and freeze. When frozen, remove and store in a labeled air-tight container.

Oatmeal Peanut Butter Muffins

350ºF

(One of these muffins will protein pack your day.)

1 1/2 c. buttermilk (1 c. for celiac)
1 2/3 c. oatmeal
1 2/3 c. whole wheat or wheat-free flour
1 tbsp. baking powder
3 tsp. baking soda
1/2 c. cleaned, dried raisins (optional)
1/2 c. liquid honey
1/2 c. natural peanut butter
1/3 c. canola oil or unsweetened applesauce
3 large eggs or equivalent egg substitute
1 tbsp. vanilla

Preheat oven to 350ºF. Pour buttermilk over oatmeal and set aside. Mix together flour, baking powder and baking soda. Stir in raisins if using. Beat together honey, peanut butter, oil or applesauce, eggs and vanilla. Add liquid mixture to dry ingredients, stirring only until blended. Fill prepared muffin tins, the size of your choice and bake accordingly. (see pg. 6)

Gluten-Free: not appropriate

Yields & Nutrient Analysis for Large & Carbohydrate-Reduced Sizes:

	Yield	Energy (Kcal)	Protein (g)	Fat (g)	Carb. (g)
Whole Wheat/Regular	13	279	9.8	13.8	28
No Added Fat	13	228	9.8	7.8	28.4
Carbohydrate-Reduced	26	114	4.9	3.9	14.2
Diabetic Food Choices	1 starch + 1/2 protein				

Nutrition TIP: Most people consider the peanut as just that — a nut; but the peanut is a legume and valued as an (incomplete) source of protein. However, when combined with a grain, as in the muffin, it then becomes a complete protein. Add a glass of milk for a wholesome snack.

103 Years Young and Still Going Strong

The year — 1890, the local-St. Louis Missouri, the event — the discovery of a still popular protein food, namely peanut butter. People were eating peanuts for over 3,500 years before a doctor discovered using them as a spread while searching for an easily digestible, nutritious food for his elderly patients.

Although he was certain this paste made by grinding peanuts would become popular, I'm sure he would be shocked at its continued popularity. According to Statistics Canada, we eat 100 million kilograms of peanut butter a year.

Many of the brands we see on our supermarket shelves today originated in the 1920's and 30's. Unfortunately, many now have added salt, fat and sugar. To avoid these undesirable ingredients, make your own, buy freshly ground or buy commercial brands that list peanuts as the only ingredient. Only then will you be sure you are enjoying this unique food the way in which the good doctor intended.

Shirley M. Hartung

🐾 🐾 🐾

Honey and Peanut butter is always a favourite combination. I think you'll enjoy this honey/peanut butter mixture.

Sweet Peanut Spread

2/3 c. creamed honey
1/2 c. peanut butter
2 tbsp. soft butter

To prepare above spread, simply beat together all ingredients until smooth.

NOTE: This spread is not low in calories so spread sparingly. It is not appropriate for diabetics.

Cranberry Orange Muffins

350°F   (no milk)

(A good Christmas muffin, but popular year round.)

4 c. whole wheat or wheat-free flour
1 tbsp. baking powder
2 tsp. baking soda
1 1/2 c. coarsely-chopped cranberries
1/2 c. coarsely-chopped walnuts (optional)
1 whole orange minced very fine
1 1/4 c. unsweetened orange juice
2/3 c. liquid honey (1/3 c. for diabetic)
1/4 c. canola oil or unsweetened applesauce
2 large eggs or equivalent egg substitute

Preheat oven to 350°F. Mix together flour, baking powder and baking soda. Stir in chopped walnuts, if using. Chop cranberries and mince orange. Beat together juice, honey, oil or applesauce and eggs. Add fruit to liquid ingredients. Add liquid mixture into dry ingredients, stirring only until blended. Fill prepared muffin tins, the size of your choice and bake accordingly. (see pg. 6)

Gluten-Free: yield 13 (using rice/starch combination, see pg. 84)

Yields & Nutrient Analysis for Large & Carbohydrate-Reduced Sizes:

	Yield	Energy (Kcal)	Protein (g)	Fat (g)	Carb. (g)
Whole Wheat/Regular	12	283	6.9	6.8	51.8
No Added Fat	12	241	6.9	2.0	52.3
Carbohydrate-Reduced	28	89	3.0	0.9	18.7
Diabetic Food Choices	1 starch				

TIP: Do not leave cranberries whole as they are much too tart. If using a food processor to blend liquids, add cranberries briefly at the end. This makes quick work to an otherwise arduous task.

DID YOU KNOW? Early North American settlers gave cranberries their name after watching 'cranes' feast on these bitter red berries.

Marmalade Orange Oatmeal Muffins

350°F

(Oatmeal with a 'hint' of marmalade.)

2 c. oatmeal
1 c. unsweetened orange juice or milk (scant 1/2 c. for gluten-free)
2 c. whole wheat or wheat-free flour
2 tsp. baking powder
2 tsp. baking soda
1/2 c. almond chunks (optional)
1 tbsp. grated orange rind (optional)
1/2 — 2/3 c. liquid honey (1/4 c. for diabetic)
1/3 c. canola oil or unsweetened applesauce (1/4 c. for diabetic)
1/2 c. marmalade (1/4 c. for diabetic)
4 large eggs or equivalent egg substitute
1 tsp. almond extract

Preheat oven to 350°F. Pour juice or milk over oatmeal and allow to soak. Meanwhile, mix together flour, baking powder and baking soda. Stir in raisins and almonds and orange rind if using. Beat together honey, oil or applesauce, marmalade, eggs and almond flavouring. Stir soaked oatmeal into liquids. Add liquid mixture to dry ingredients, stirring only until blended. Fill prepared muffin tins, the size of your choice and bake accordingly. (see pg. 6)

Gluten-Free: yield 11 (using the "Gluten-Free Anytime" Baking Mix, see pg. 84 and rice cereal)

Yields & Nutrient Analysis for Large & Carbohydrate-Reduced Sizes:

	Yield	Energy (Kcal)	Protein (g)	Fat (g)	Carb. (g)
Whole Wheat/Regular	12	295	7.8	10	46.8
No Added Fat	12	240	7.8	3.6	47.3
Carbohydrate-Reduced	23	108	4.0	3.9	20.2
Diabetic Food Choices	1 starch + 1/2 fruits/vegetables				

Orange Apricot Muffins (H.F.)

350ºF
(This muffin gives you a double dose of Vitamin 'C'.)

1 c. unsweetened orange juice (1/2 c. for gluten-free)
1/2 c. cleaned, chopped, dried apricots
grated rind of 1 orange
4 c. whole wheat or wheat-free flour
1 tbsp. baking powder
1 tsp. baking soda
1/2 c. cleaned, dried raisins (1/4 c. for diabetic)
1/2 c. sliced almonds (optional)
1 1/2 c. buttermilk or sour milk
1/2 — 2/3 c. liquid honey (1/4 c. for diabetic)
1/4 c. canola oil or unsweetened applesauce
2 large eggs or equivalent egg substitute
1 tsp. almond extract

Preheat oven to 350ºF. Chop cleaned apricots. Soak minced peel and apricots in orange juice. In another bowl, mix together flour, baking powder and baking soda. Stir in raisins and almonds if using. Beat together milk, honey, oil or applesauce, eggs and extract. Add liquid mixture to dry ingredients, stirring only until blended. Fill prepared muffin tins, the size of your choice and bake accordingly. (see pg. 6)

Gluten-Free: yield 12 (using rice/cornstarch combination, see pg. 84)

Yields & Nutrient Analysis for Large & Carbohydrate-Reduced Sizes:

	Yield	Energy (Kcal)	Protein (g)	Fat (g)	Carb. (g)
Whole Wheat/Regular	15	252	7.0	5.6	47.1
No Added Fat	13	253	8.1	2.1	54.8
Carbohydrate-Reduced	29	97	3.5	20.2	0.9
Diabetic Food Choices	1 starch + 1/2 fruits/vegetables				

Orange Currant Muffins

350°F — 25 minutes for mega size   (no milk variation)
(A scone-like muffin.)

3 1/2 c. whole wheat or wheat-free flour
2 tbsp. baking powder
1 c. washed, dried currants
1 grated rind of a large orange
1 1/3 — 1 1/2 c. milk or orange juice (1 c. for wheat-free, 1 1/3 for gluten-free)
1/4 — 1/3 c. canola oil or unsweetened applesauce
2 large eggs or equivalent egg substitute
1/2 c. liquid honey (1/4 c. for diabetic)

Preheat oven to 350°F. Mix together flour and baking powder. Stir in raisins and grated orange rind. Beat together juice or milk, oil or applesauce, eggs and honey. Add liquid mixture to dry ingredients, stirring only until blended. Fill prepared muffin tins, the size of your choice and bake accordingly. (see pg. 6)

Gluten-Free: yield 10 (using light buckwheat and tapioca in the same ratio as rice/starch combination, see pg. 84)

Yields & Nutrient Analysis for Large & Carbohydrate-Reduced Sizes:

	Yield	Energy (Kcal)	Protein (g)	Fat (g)	Carb. (g)
Whole Wheat/Regular	10	319	8.1	8.0	58.3
No Added Fat	10	271	8.1	2.3	58.9
Carbohydrate-Reduced	26	96	3.1	0.9	20.5
Diabetic Food Choices					

Walnut Orange Date Muffins

350°F   (no milk)
(This muffin reminds me of my Grandmother's date-orange cake.)

4 1/2 c. whole wheat or wheat-free flour
1 tbsp. baking powder
2 tsp. baking soda
1/2 c. coarsely-chopped walnuts (optional)
1 whole large orange, finely minced
1 c. cleaned, chopped dates (1/2 c. for diabetic)
1 3/4 c. unsweetened orange juice
1/2 c. canola oil or unsweetened applesauce
3/4 c. liquid honey (1/3 c. for diabetic)
4 large eggs or equivalent egg substitute

Preheat oven to 350°F. Mix together flour, baking powder and baking soda. Stir in walnuts if using, minced orange and dates. Beat together juice, oil or applesauce, honey and eggs. Add liquid mixture to dry ingredients, stirring only until blended. Fill prepared muffin tins, the size of your choice and bake accordingly. (see pg. 6)

Gluten-Free: yield 15 (using rice/cornstarch combination, see pg. 84, plus 2 tsp. guar gum.)

Yields & Nutrient Analysis for Large & Carbohydrate-Reduced Sizes:

	Yield	Energy (Kcal)	Protein (g)	Fat (g)	Carb. (g)
Whole Wheat/Regular	18	270	6.1	8.4	45.8
No Added Fat	18	216	6.1	2.1	46.7
Carbohydrate-Reduced	35	90	3.1	1.1	18.3
Diabetic Food Choices	1 starch				

Sticky Recollections

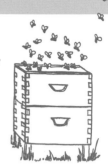

No work? Not feel like dancing? Neither does the honey bee during a dry season. Drought to the honey bee is like a recession to us because there is little work.

Scouter bees locate the source of nectar and communicate this to the worker bees by a special dance on the honeycomb. If there is little nectar, there is little dancing and little work so the bees just stay at home.

My earliest childhood memory about honey is a sticky one. I knocked over a five pound pail just after Dad had arrived home from the bee-keepers with our fall supply. Since it was fresh honey, it was very runny. Mother still reminds me what a terrible mess it was to clean up.

Little did I realize at the time, the work I had destroyed, given the fact that a bee would have to visit about seven million flowers and fly a distance equal to three times around the earth to produce one pound of honey — never mind five pounds.

As I re-fill my pails with my fall supply of honey, I am now more conscious of the work involved. I am particularly careful when filling my five-pound pail.

🐝 🐝 🐝

Although I don't usually use a recipe for cinnamon honey butter, I have included one as a guide for your use:

Cinnamon Honey Butter

    1/2 c. soft butter
    1/2 c. creamed honey
    1 tbsp. cinnamon

To prepare above spread, simply beat together all ingredients until smooth.

Note: This spread is not low in calories. Spread sparingly. It is not appropriate for diabetics.

Butter Pecan Muffins

375°F

(This muffin is plain but wonderfully rich.)

4 c. whole wheat or wheat-free flour
1 tbsp. baking powder
2 tsp. baking soda
3/4 c. chopped pecans
1 1/2 c. low-fat milk
1/2 c. liquid honey
1/2 c. melted butter (use a good quality margarine, if butter not
    allowed)
4 large eggs or equivalent egg substitute
2 tsp. vanilla

Preheat oven to 375°F. Mix together flour, baking powder and baking soda. Stir in pecans. Beat together milk, honey, butter, eggs and vanilla. Add liquid mixture to dry ingredients, stirring only until blended. Fill prepared muffin tins, the size of your choice and bake accordingly. (see pg. 6)

TIP: Top each muffin with a whole pecan before baking.

Gluten-Free: not appropriate

Yields & Nutrient Analysis for Large & Carbohydrate-Reduced Sizes:

	Yield	Energy (Kcal)	Protein (g)	Fat (g)	Carb. (g)
Whole Wheat/Regular	12	336	9.4	16.1	42.6
No Added Fat	N/A	—	—	—	—
Carbohydrate-Reduced	N/A	—	—	—	—
Diabetic Food Choices					

Mandarin Date Mango Muffins

350ºF   (no milk)

(This muffin has a touch of the exotic.)

3 c. whole wheat or wheat-free flour
2 c. fine oatmeal
1 tbsp. baking powder
3 tsp. baking soda
1/2 c. unsweetened coconut
1 c. unsweetened orange juice
1/2 c. liquid honey (1/4 c. for diabetic)
1/4 — 1/2 c. canola oil or unsweetened applesauce
2 large eggs or equivalent egg substitute
1 tsp. almond extract
1 c. chopped, ripe mango (1 large mango)
1 c. mandarin orange pieces (1-10 oz. can drained)
1/2 c. washed, chopped dates (1/4 c. for diabetic)

Preheat oven to 350ºF. Mix together flour, oatmeal, baking powder, and baking soda. Stir in coconut. Beat together juice honey, oil or applesauce, eggs and almond extract. Stir fruit into liquid mixture. Add liquid mixture to dry ingredients, stirring only until blended. Fill prepared muffin tins, the size of your choice and bake accordingly. (see pg. 6)

Gluten-Free: yield 17 (using bean flour as you would rice & cornstarch combination, see pg. 84 and rice cereal)
Add two extra cups of juice.

Yields & Nutrient Analysis for Large & Carbohydrate-Reduced Sizes:

	Yield	Energy (Kcal)	Protein (g)	Fat (g)	Carb. (g)
Whole Wheat/Regular	14	274	6.9	7.6	47.7
No Added Fat	14	241	6.9	3.6	48.8
Carbohydrate-Reduced	31	99	3.1	1.6	19.3
Diabetic Food Choices	1 starch + 1/2 fruits/vegetables				

Maple Walnut Muffins

375°F

(Maple syrup brings a hint of spring to this recipe!)

2 c. buttermilk
2 tsp. baking soda
4 c. whole wheat or wheat-free flour
1 tbsp. baking powder
1 c. walnut pieces (reserve some for topping or use whole walnuts
    for a special occasion)
3/4 c. pure maple syrup
1/3 c. canola oil or unsweetened applesauce
3 large eggs or equivalent egg substitute
2 tsp. maple extract

Preheat oven to 375°F. Stir baking soda into buttermilk and set aside. Mix flour and baking powder together. Stir in walnuts. Beat together maple syrup, oil or applesauce, eggs and maple extract. Blend soda/buttermilk mixture into liquids. Add liquid mixture to dry ingredients, stirring only until blended. Fill prepared muffin tins, the size of your choice and bake accordingly. (see pg. 6)

Gluten-Free: not appropriate

Yields & Nutrient Analysis for Large & Carbohydrate-Reduced Sizes:

	Yield	Energy (Kcal)	Protein (g)	Fat (g)	Carb. (g)
Whole Wheat/Regular	12	345	10	14.8	47.6
No Added Fat	N/A	—	—	—	—
Carbohydrate-Reduced	29	120	4.1	3.4	20.0
Diabetic Food Choices	1 starch + 1/2 fruits/vegetables				

TIP: For a special occasion, glaze warm muffins with maple syrup or serve warm with maple butter. For a special "sweet treat" visit our famous Waterloo Farmers' Market and buy yourself a jar of maple jelly.

Think Spring

In our area, the tapping of maple trees in preparation for the annual Elmira Maple Syrup Festival heralds the spring. A combination of warm, sunny days and frosty nights is needed to make the sap run.

After the sap is collected it is boiled until it becomes syrup. It takes about forty gallons of sap to make one gallon of syrup so each drop is precious.

Thousands of hungry people flock here each year for the taste of hot pancakes and "real" maple syrup.

Our forefathers learned to make maple syrup from the Indians. For them it was a staple food. At their sugar camps, sap was collected in bark buckets and heated to boiling over red hot coals, in hollowed-out logs. Until European settlers arrived bringing their iron kettles, this was a long labourious job. I remember collecting sap from the maple grove at the back of our farm and then boiling it down into syrup. It was work, but you really felt in touch with nature.

The pale, clear sap from the first cooking has the most delicate flavour, so it is preferred for pouring over pancakes and fritters. The darker, stronger flavoured syrup which comes later in the season is best for baking.

Maple butter, syrup cooked to a spreading consistency, is my favourite. Spread on warm toast, tea-biscuits or muffins it is nature at its best.

$ Million Dollar Muffins $

350ºF   (no milk)
(An expensive special occasion muffin.)

2 1/2 c. whole wheat or wheat free flour
3/4 c. oatmeal (double for wheat-free)
3/4 c. wheat germ (omit for wheat-free)
1 tbsp. baking powder
1 tbsp. baking soda
1/2 c. candied papaya
1/2 c. candied pineapple
1/2 c. pepitas (green pumpkin seeds)
1/2 c. unsweetened coconut
1/2 c. cleaned, chopped dates
1 c. unsweetened pineapple juice
1/2 — 3/4 c. liquid honey
1/2 c. (scant) canola oil or unsweetened applesauce
3 large eggs or equivalent egg substitute
2 tsp. almond extract

Preheat oven to 350ºF. Mix together flour, oatmeal, wheat germ if using, baking powder and baking soda. Stir in candied fruits and seeds. Beat together juice, honey, oil or applesauce, eggs and flavouring. Add liquid mixture to dry ingredients, stirring only until blended. Fill prepared muffin tins, the size of your choice and bake accordingly. (see pg. 6)

Gluten-Free: not appropriate

Yields & Nutrient Analysis for Large & Carbohydrate-Reduced Sizes:

	Yield	Energy (Kcal)	Protein (g)	Fat (g)	Carb. (g)
Whole Wheat/Regular	12	483	11.3	21.3	65.6
No Added Fat	12	398	11.3	11.8	66.1
Carbohydrate-Reduced	N/A	—	—	—	—
Diabetic Food Choices					

Polka-Dot Banana Muffins

350°F   (no milk)

(A nice Christmas morning muffin.)

2 1/2 c. whole wheat or wheat-free flour
4 tsp. baking powder
1 c. diced baking gums (1-8oz. package), do not use black gums
1/2 c. washed, dried raisins
1/4 c. chopped nuts of your choice
1/2 c. unsweetened orange juice
1/2 c. liquid honey
1/3 c. canola oil or unsweetened applesauce
3 large eggs or equivalent egg substitute
1/2 c. mashed, ripe banana (1 banana)

Preheat oven to 350°F. Mix together flour and baking powder. Stir in gums, raisins and nuts. Beat together juice, honey, oil or applesauce and eggs. Mash banana and add to liquid mixture. Add liquid mixture to dry ingredients, stirring only till blended. Fill prepared muffin tins, the size of your choice and bake accordingly. (see pg. 6)

Gluten-Free: not appropriate

Yields & Nutrient Analysis for Large & Carbohydrate-Reduced Sizes:

	Yield	Energy (Kcal)	Protein (g)	Fat (g)	Carb. (g)
Whole Wheat/Regular	9	363	7.3	11.4	62.0
No Added Fat	10	263	6.6	2.6	57.0
Carbohydrate-Reduced	N/A	—	—	—	—
Diabetic Food Choices					

kiwi Granola Muffins (H.F.)

375°F
(A conversation piece!)

1 c. buttermilk
1 tbsp. baking soda
1 1/2 c. natural bran
2 c. whole wheat flour
2 c. homemade granola (see pg. 75)
1 tbsp. baking powder
1/2 tsp. cinnamon
1 1/2 c. coarsely-chopped kiwi fruit (4 to 6 kiwi)
1/2 c. liquid honey (1/3 c. for diabetic)
1/4 c. canola oil or unsweetened applesauce
3 large eggs or equivalent substitute

Preheat oven to 375°F. Stir baking soda into buttermilk and set aside.
Mix together bran, flour, granola, baking powder and cinnamon. Stir in
kiwi. Beat together honey, oil or applesauce and eggs. Stir into
buttermilk. Add liquid mixture to dry ingredients, stirring only until
blended. Fill prepared muffin tins, the size of your choice and bake
accordingly. (see pg. 6)

Gluten-Free: not appropriate

Yields & Nutrient Analysis for Large & Carbohydrate-Reduced Sizes:

	Yield	Energy (Kcal)	Protein (g)	Fat (g)	Carb. (g)
Whole Wheat/Regular	12	295	7.8	12.0	43.8
No Added Fat	13	235	7.2	6.6	40.8
Carbohydrate-Reduced	28	104	3.4	3.1	17.6
Diabetic Food Choices	1 starch				

DID YOU KNOW? Thousands of years before the kiwi was domesticated and
cultivated, it grew wild in China's Yangtse River Valley. Although it was
introduced into New Zealand in the early 1900's, it was still virtually unknown
twenty years ago. Later it was cultivated to become the larger, juicier version
that we know today. This so-called "new fruit" was renamed, because of its
resemblance to New Zealand's National bird, the small, brown, flightless kiwi.

NUTRITION TIP: There is not a more concentrated source of Vitamin C,
calorie for calorie than the kiwi fruit and it provides 224% of the
recommended daily intake of Vitamin C. It is also a source of fibre, is high in
potassium and one kiwi has only 47 calories. To ripen, store at room
temperature 3-5 days. Place in a bag with an apple or banana to hasten
ripening.

Granola (H.F.)

300ºF   (no milk, no eggs)
(A nutritious breakfast cereal.)

14 c. large oats or a substitute
2 c. wheat germ
2 c. oat bran
2 c. unsweetened coconut
1 c. raw, unsalted sesame seeds
1 c. raw, unsalted sunflower seeds
1 tbsp. pure vanilla
1 c. good quality oil (canola, sunflower, safflower, etc.)
1 c. liquid honey

Preheat oven to 300ºF. Mix all dry ingredients in a very large bowl. Stir in oil and honey. Spread this about 1 inch deep in 2 large pans. Bake for 1/2 hour or until golden, on the middle rack of your oven, stirring every 10 to 15 minutes. Cool. Add 1 cup raisins or chopped dates and 1 cup dried apple pieces. One cup sliced almonds is lovely, but optional. If you like chunky granola, leave it undisturbed overnight to cool and then stir in dried fruit.

Unsweetened Variation — replace honey with 1 can frozen, unsweetened, undiluted apple or pineapple juice. Bake as above. This is a very non-sweet but satisfying breakfast meal.

Gluten-free Variation — replace oats with puffed rice, omit wheat germ and oat bran and replace with extra puffed rice. This is for eating as breakfast cereal, not to be used in muffins. I like the crunch!

Diabetic — remove dried fruits.

Yields & Nutrient Analysis for Large & Carbohydrate-Reduced Sizes:

	Yield	Energy (Kcal)	Protein (g)	Fat (g)	Carb. (g)
Whole Wheat/Regular	26	458	10.1	28	41.9
No Added Fat	N/A	—	—	—	—
Carbohydrate-Reduced	12	230	5.0	15	18
Diabetic Food Choices	1 starch, 1 protein + 3 fat/oils				

To lower fat content reduce coconut and sesame seeds by half.

🌿 Nutrient Analysis based on 1/2 cup of Granola.

Homemade Mincemeat

4 c. chopped green tomato (about 6 tomatoes)
4 c. chopped apples (about 6 cooking apples)
1 c. currants
1 c. raisins
3 tsp. ground cinnamon
1 tsp. ground cloves
1/2 tsp. allspice
1/2 tsp. ground ginger
1/4 c. vinegar
1 tbsp. grated orange peel
1/2 c. unsweetened orange juice

(Try pears if you don't have green tomatoes.)

Combine all ingredients in a large heavy pot. Simmer until thick.

Yields & Nutrient Analysis for Large & Carbohydrate-Reduced Sizes:

	Yield	Energy (Kcal)	Protein (g)	Fat (g)	Carb. (g)
Whole Wheat/Regular	7	132	1.8	0.6	34.0
No Added Fat	7	132	1.8	0.6	34.0
Carbohydrate-Reduced	7	132	1.8	0.6	34.0
Diabetic Food Choices	N/A				

Nutrient Analysis based on 1 cup of mincemeat.

Museli

A nutritious grain/nut/seed cereal of Swiss origin boasts oatmeal as its main ingredient, as does granola. Oats have the highest protein content of all the grains. In museli, the oat mixture is soaked in water or juice overnight and then is eaten raw, often topped with yogurt. A combination of dried fruits, nuts and seeds are part of the mixture. Sliced almonds, as well as sunflower, sesame and pumpkin seeds are popular additions. Museli is similar to granola but is not toasted.

> 3 c. rolled oats (or 4 c. rice cereal for gluten-free)
> 1 c. cleaned raisins or currants or 1/2 c. of each
> 1 c. cleaned dates
> 1 c. sliced almonds
> 1 c. sunflower seeds
> 1 c. sesame seeds
> 1 c. unsweetened coconut (optional)

Mix all ingredients together and store tightly sealed.

Yields & Nutrient Analysis for Large & Carbohydrate-Reduced Sizes:

	Yield	Energy (Kcal)	Protein (g)	Fat (g)	Carb. (g)
Whole Wheat/Regular	9	565	17.8	32	60
No Added Fat	9	565	17.8	32	60
Carbohydrate-Reduced	9c.	287	9	16	30
Diabetic Food Choices	2 starches + 1 protein + 3 fat/oils				

To lower fat content reduce coconut and sesame seeds by half.

🥄 Nutrient Analysis based on 1/2 cup of museli.

TIP: Store sunflower seeds in the refrigerator to prevent rancidity. Sunflower seeds are a good source of iron, zinc and Vitamin C.

DID YOU KNOW? To prevent soldiers from starving during Czarist wars, each soldier, before going to the battlefield, was given a bag of sunflower seeds. This was called "his" iron ration. Sunflower seeds have 12 different minerals, 17 vitamins, protein and polyunsaturated oil.

Substitutions

Eggs

1/3 c. flax seed (ground or left whole)
1 c. water

Bring above mixture to boil. Simmer 3 minutes. (Do not over cook or use too high a temperature or the mixture will become thick and gummy). Refrigerate and use within a short period of time. One tbsp. of this mixture is equal to one egg. This egg replacement will bind but not leaven.

Other choices to replace one egg, include using:

- 2 egg whites
- or 2 ounces of tofu
- or 1/3 c. apple juice
- or 2 tbsp. pureed apricot
- or 2 tbsp. baking powder + 2 tbsp. liquid + 1 tbsp. oil
- or 1 tsp. Xanthan gum = 1-2 eggs

Milk and Dairy

Many people have problems with milk. As much as 70% of the world population is reported to be lactose intolerant. (Lactose is the main sugar in milk.) Some people are also sensitive to the protein in milk.

Lacteeze And Lactaid:
These are commercial products for the lactose intolerant. This milk has all (99%) or part of the lactose predigested. Check the label for this information. Lactaid always has 99% of the lactose predigested. Both come in skim and 2%. The skim is slightly sweeter and has a fuller taste compared with regular skim milk due to the effect of the natural enzyme that is added to convert the lactose into a digestible form. For most people 5 drops of Lactaid are sufficient for a litre of milk but to make the lactose 99% predigested, 15 drops per litre is required. Always allow the milk to refrigerate 24 hours for the process to be completed. Lactaid can be used in cream as well but is not effective in yogurt. Lactaid pills are also available at the pharmacy and can be

taken before consuming dairy products to offset the negative effects some people experience from consuming dairy products.

Tofu White:

A powdered form of tofu (soybean curd) is made into a milk by reconstituting it by mixing it with water. Use approx. 9 tablespoons of powder to 4 cups water, or as directed. If using a blender, all cold water may be used, however, if stirring by hand, use half hot water first to dissolve the powder, then add the remaining cold water. This milk substitute is fortified with B12 and if served cold is a good alternate to milk. It has no lactose and ounce for ounce, it has more calcium than milk. Tofu has no cholesterol either, and since it is made from soybeans, which are mostly protein, it acts like dairy. It has been compared by nutritionists, to lean meats for its protein value. Tofu white when reconstituted makes a nice white milk substitute.

Nut Milks:

To save time, buy nuts without the skins. If this is too expensive, pour boiling water over the nuts to loosen the skins. Let sit briefly until they slip off easily. Do not let them cool or the skins will tighten again. Use approximately 20 almonds per c. of water, depending on how rich a milk you wish. Process well in food processor or blender, strain (save grindings, dry and use in cookie batter, etc.)

Cashew Milk:

Prepare as for almond milk. Be aware however, that almonds have more calcium.

Goat's Milk:

It is now available in powdered and evaporated form as well as in liquid form. The fat gobules are smaller than those in cow's milk so are therefore easier to digest. Goat's milk does however have lactose, as does cow's milk, so therefore is not a good choice for those with a lactose intolerance, unless Lactaid is used.

Soy Milk:

It can be purchased commercially. I understand that children are particularly fond of the flavoured varieties.

Fruit Milk:

Liquefy a banana, then add 2-3 c. of your favourite unsweetened juice, (pineapple is best) and blend again. Make only what is required or stir a little Vitamin C (ascorbic acid) over left-overs before refrigerating to prevent the mixture from darkening.

Honey, maple syrup, unsweetened juices, dried or fresh fruits, barley malt, apple syrup, rice syrup and fruit source.

Malt Syrup:
Available from health food stores, it is made from barley. It is not a good choice for the yeast sensitive as it is a fermented product. In fact it will continue to ferment if left at room temperature, so it must be refrigerated. As it becomes very thick when cold it must be brought to room temperature before using or it will be too difficult to work with.

Apple Syrup:
It is an apple concentrate and like applebutter has no sugar added. It is available at most grocery stores under the Wellesley Label. It can, like malt syrup, replace corn syrup in a recipe. I have tested all the recipes in this book with apple syrup as well as with honey. Most were acceptable with the apple syrup except for those with a more delicate flavour, in which case the apple flavour was overpowering.

Rice Syrup:
A natural sweetener made from rice, it does not have the same intensity of sweetness as do the other sweeteners listed, however it may be preferred by some because of this. I also find that baked goods do not bake as golden in colour.

Fruit Source:
A relatively new sweetener alternative, fruit source can be purchased in both liquid and powder or crystal form. It is made from a combination of grape juice concentrate and whole rice syrup and is used to replace other sweeteners including honey. It is claimed to have superior moisture retaining qualities, so as a consequence 50% less fats and oils are needed. It tastes like sugar so is an ideal sugar substitute, however, it is relatively expensive.

Splenda:
It is the latest low-calorie sweetener actually created from sugar. It only has 2 calories/tsp., so has only a fraction of the calories in sugar. It comes in granular form and replaces sugar spoon for spoon. It can be used in baking because of its incredible heat stability. As some baked good do not bake as deep a golden colour, check for doneness 5–10 minutes earlier than if you were using sugar.

I have tested the recipes in this book using Splenda, as I was curious what adjustments would be required when replacing honey. I was surprised that in most recipes no additional liquid was required. In the odd recipe, adding a tbsp. or two of liquid did help to make the batter less stiff to stir, however, adding the dry ingredients to the liquid mixture a cup at a time also helped overcome this problem.

Splenda is appropriate for people on a calorie-reduced or sugar-free diet. Because of the low calorie count I was able to replace the highest amount of honey suggested in the recipes with Splenda and still stay within the guidelines for a diabetic.

Citrus

If sensitive to lemon, you may be able to use Vitamin C powder in its place. To replace 1 tablespoon lemon juice, use 1/4 tsp. Vitamin powder and 1 tbsp. water.

Oatmeal

Use any of these flaked products that you can tolerate: barley flakes, rye flakes, spelt flakes or rice flakes. As rice flakes are hard to find, I have substituted oatmeal in gluten-free recipes with rice cereal. (this is not a commercial boxed cereal)

Bran

Oat bran, (I have also used oatmeal or a combination of oatbran and oatmeal if the amount of wheat bran being replaced is a large amount). Rice bran is another option, but personally I am not fond of this product. Use it only in small amounts as it soaks up a lot of the liquid resulting in a dry product.

Wheat Germ

Sesame seed flour may be used in small amounts. Corn Germ, another relatively new product, has twice as much fibre as wheat germ and is high in important vitamins and minerals. The texture is crunchy, compared to wheat germ.

Flour

(use cup for cup unless otherwise stated)

Wheat-Free Flour:
This flour combination of equal amounts of rye, oat and barley is available pre-mixed. However if you are sensitive to one of these grains you will have to mix your own replacing the offending grain with one you can tolerate. Spelt is safe for most wheat-sensitive people.

Oat Flour:
It also can be purchased pre-mixed or you can make your own. You will need 1 1/4 c. fine oats to yield one cup oat flour. Oat flour is highly nutritious.

Buckwheat Flour:
It is often advised to mix buckwheat flour with other flours such as rice to lighten it as it tends to be a heavier flour. Another possible combination for the wheat sensitive is to use equal amounts of millet, barley and arrowroot.

Amaranth Flour:
A seed, not a grain, this flour is expensive, but I would use it for special occasion celiac baking. Combine amaranth with rice flour or a starch as suggested below. 25% amaranth and 75% brown rice flour or 75% amaranth and 25% arrowroot, tapioca or potato starch.

Quinola Flour:
An ancient grain, Quinola, is a complete protein and also has all the essential amino acids in a balanced pattern. It can be made into a finely ground flour which has a nutty flavour. It is know for building strength and endurance because of its high protein content. It also contains the B Vitamins, iron, fibre, calcium and phosphorous. As with amaranth and buckwheat, it can be tolerated by most people allergic to various cereal grains.

Almond Flour:
It is made from ground almonds, so it too is expensive. Store in the refrigerator. Let the batter sit for half an hour before baking to improve the texture.

Chickpea Flour:
It may be used in small amounts to add protein to baked goods. Replace only 1/4 of the total amount of flour with chickpea flour.

Corn Flour:

If not sensitive to corn, corn flour may be used for variety in a gluten-free diet.

Millet Flour:

It is well balanced in essential amino acids. It has more iron than any other cereal. To greatly increase the protein utilization of millet, use with legumes. (Spread peanut butter on your millet muffin). Millet lacks gluten so it is appropriate for a celiac. It is the most easily digested of all cereals. Millet is not a grain, but belongs to a group of small-seeded grasses.

Buckwheat:

It is one of the few commercially cultivated crops not routinely sprayed with pesticides. Buckwheat is rich in potassium, phosphorus and the B Vitamins. It is the best natural source of a complex plant material called rutic acid which is said to be helpful for circulation problems.

Rice Flour:

Brown rice flour is considered the least allergic of all the grains. It has a structure similar to that of wheat and like wheat, looses valuable nutrition when the outer layers are removed in milling. The first clue to Vitamin B was found when thousands of Japanese sailors died when the Japanese navy began to use polished rice. Rice has the nutrients of all the cereal grains plus calcium, Vitamin B6 (pantothenic acid) and Vitamin K. The bran and germ also contain phosphorus, iron, Vitamin E and most of the B Vitamins. It is an incomplete protein as it is lacking in the amino acid lysine. The above description refers to brown rice. White rice has the bran removed so the vitamin and mineral content is drastically reduced. The protein is also reduced. Enriching only partially replaces these losses.

Formulas for Gluten-free Combinations

Rice combinations and Ratios
7/8 c. rice flour = 1 c. whole wheat flour
7/8 c. = 1 level c. minus 2 tbsp. or 3/4 + 1/8 c.

Combining Rice and (Cornstarch, Arrowroot or Potato Starch)
Use 75% flour and 25% starch
For your convenience: to replace another flour with rice and a starch use these formulas:

- for 2 c. of flour use: 1 1/2 c. rice flour + 1/2 c. starch
- for 3 c. of flour use: 2 1/4 c. rice flour and 3/4 c. starch
- for 3 1/2 c. of flour use: 2 1/2 + 1/8 or 2 5/8 c. rice flour + 3/4 c + 1/8 or 7/8 c. starch
- for 4 c. of flour use: 3 c. rice flour + 1 c. starch
- for 4 1/2 c. flour use: 3 1/4 + 1/8 c rice flour + 1 1/8 c. starch
- for 5 c. flour use: 3 3/4 c. rice flour and 1 1/4 c. starch

Recipes where I have used rice flour and a starch in this book have used the above formulas. You may have another formula or may wish to use the formula below taken from "Diet For Life" with permission from the Celiac Association. Be advised however that the yields may vary:
5/8 c. rice flour + 1/3 c. potato starch.
3/4 c. rice flour + 1/4 c. cornstarch

Homemade Flour Mix — "Gluten-Free Anytime" Baking Mix
3 c. white rice flour
1 c. brown rice flour
2 c. potato starch
1 c. cornstarch
1 c. soy flour

Sift, then measure each amount of flour and starch. Combine well and store in an airtight container in a cool dry place. This recipe is printed with permission of the authors of *"Gluten-Free Anytime,"* an excellent book for those requiring gluten-free recipes. If you are interested in purchasing a copy of this cookbook write to Gluten-free Anytime, 3429-136 Ave., Edmonton, Alberta T5A2W5 for more information.

Baking Powder

Gluten-Free Baking Powder:

1 part baking soda
2 parts cornstarch
2 parts cream of tartar

Sample
1 c. baking soda
2 c. cornstarch
2 c. cream of tartar

❧ Sift very well.

(printed from *"Diet for Life"* with permission of the Celiac Association.)

Corn-Free Baking Powder:
(For celiacs also allergic to corn.) Use equal amounts of baking soda, potato starch and cream of tartar
Sample
1/4 c. baking soda
1/4 c. potato starch
1/4 c. cream of tartar

Aluminum-Free Baking Powder:
1/4 c. baking soda
1/2 cream of tartar
1/2 c. arrowroot flour

Low-Sodium Baking Powder:
Replace baking soda in recipe above with potassium bicarbonate (available at a pharmacy)

I like to suggest using low sodium, aluminum-free baking powder as it contains 1 mg of sodium per tsp. compared with 40 mg per tsp. in regular baking powder. This can be purchased commercially.

Metric Conversions

1 tbsp. (tbsp. or T.) ....15 ml
1 tsp. (tsp. or t.) ....5 ml
1/2 tsp...2.4 ml or 2 ml
1/4 tsp. ....1.25 ml or 1 ml
1 (generous) c. ....250 ml
1/2 (generous) c...125 ml
1/4 (scant) c. ....50 ml

Metric Weights

1 oz. ....30 g	1 lb. ....500 g
1/4 lb..........................100 g	1 1/4 lb. ....600 g
1/3 lb..........................150 g	1 1/2 lb. ....700 g
1/2 lb..........................250 g	1 3/4 lb. ....800 g
3/4 lb..........................350 g	2 lb. ....900 g

Oven Temperatures:

325°F .... 160°C (slow)
350°F .... 180°C (moderate)
375°F .... 190°C (moderate)
400°F .... 200°C (high)

Nutrient Analysis

Carb. = carbohydrate
Kcal   = calorie